Praise for *Humble Leadership*

"Effective leadership is all about building trust and relationships. With *Humble Leadership*, Ed and Peter help us actually get there by understanding relationships on a much more granular and tangible level."
—**Severin Schwan, CEO, Roche Group**

"In an era of national cynicism and dismay, this call for empathy, trust, and collaboration is a timely breath of fresh air with relevance for leaders at all levels."
—**Lucian Leape, Adjunct Professor of Health Policy (retired), Harvard School of Public Health**

"In focusing on 'levels of relationships,' the book explains how emerging leaders can succeed by interacting with peers and those reporting to them in ways that are in stark contrast to the coercive and 'bad behaviors' we are currently hearing about. Ed and Peter Schein offer an alternative and far superior approach to leadership—one based on cooperative relationships with others that emphasize trust and respect and, in turn, lead to stronger and more effective organizations."
—**Robert A. Cooke, author of Human Synergistics' *Organizational Culture Inventory***

"For those in the health-care world who face the challenge of leading organizations with layers of administrative and clinical complexity, this book offers a path to success. Humble leadership, as the authors remind us, though, is no mere philosophy. It is a result of disciplined attention to structure, culture, and relationships. The Scheins offer a persuasive road map to achieve this understanding and true effectiveness in institutional settings."
—**Paul F. Levy, former CEO, Beth Israel Deaconess Medical Center, and author of *Goal Play!***

"Humility may be the modern leader's most important attribute. In a complex, dynamic world, humility is simply realism. This powerful and thoroughly engaging book delivers the wisdom of Edgar Schein's half century of research and practice dedicated to helping organizations and those who manage them. Its authors—a pioneering organizational scholar and his son—embody humility as they describe its power in transforming organizations. Compelling case studies clarify the humble leadership approach and make it actionable."
—**Amy C. Edmondson, Novartis Professor of Leadership and Management, Harvard Business School**

"Edgar and Peter Schein's new book, *Humble Leadership*, builds on decades of study focused on organizational culture and leadership. The authors articulate the criticality of leadership in successful organizations and the strong correlation of relationships that go beyond the transactional with successful leaders and successful organizations. This is a must-read for reflective leaders at all levels seeking to enhance their effectiveness and execution in pursuit of their organizational mission and vision."

—Gary S. Kaplan, MD, Chairman and CEO, Virginia Mason Health System, and Chairman Lucian Leape Institute

"Edgar and Peter Schein have built on a series of previous informative books such as *Helping* and *Humble Inquiry* with their new book, *Humble Leadership*. The insights into the importance of relationships and building an atmosphere of openness and trust are helpful to all leaders. I believe it is particularly informative for those in health care, dealing with the marked technical and operational complexities."

—Lane F. Donnelly, MD, Chief Quality Officer, Lucile Packard Children's Hospital Stanford, and Professor, Stanford University School of Medicine

"*Humble Leadership* introduces a new model for leadership that supports effectiveness in a rapidly changing world where leaders and their followers are being driven by deeply entrenched cultural norms. The timeless insights about relationships, personizing, group process, and culture will help every leader."

—Tim Kuppler, Director of Culture and Organization Development, Human Synergistics, and cofounder of CultureUniversity.com

"The book offers a deeply human approach to leadership that is attuned to the staggering complexity, rapid change, and uncertainty facing anyone aiming to make a difference in today's world. Written as a joint project by Ed Schein and his son Peter, *Humble Leadership* is a way of being a leader that relies not on transactional power but on the relational power that comes from trust, openness, and collaboration. Illustrated with rich case examples from the Scheins' extensive practices as organizational consultants and exercises to develop leadership capacities of one's own, the book has the ring of authenticity that comes from the hearts of people who have walked the walk."

—Maureen O'Hara, Founding Fellow, International Futures Forum; Professor, National University; and coauthor, with Graham Leicester, of *Dancing at the Edge*

Humble Leadership

THE HUMBLE LEADERSHIP SERIES

- Humble Leadership
- Humble Consulting
- Humble Inquiry
- Helping

Humble Leadership

The Power of Relationships, Openness, and Trust

EDGAR H. SCHEIN
and
PETER A. SCHEIN

Berrett–Koehler Publishers, Inc.
a BK Business book

Berrett-Koehler Publishers, Inc.
1333 Broadway, Suite 1000
Oakland, CA 94612-1921
Tel: (510) 817-2277
Fax: (510) 817-2278
www.bkconnection.com

ORDERING INFORMATION

Quantity sales. Special discounts are available on quantity purchases by corporations, associations, and others. For details, contact the "Special Sales Department" at the Berrett-Koehler address above.

Individual sales. Berrett-Koehler publications are available through most bookstores. They can also be ordered directly from Berrett-Koehler: Tel: (800) 929-2929; Fax: (802) 864-7626; www.bkconnection.com.

Orders for college textbook/course adoption use. Please contact Berrett-Koehler: Tel: (800) 929-2929; Fax: (802) 864-7626.

Distributed to the US trade and internationally by Penguin Random House Publisher Services.

Berrett-Koehler and the BK logo are registered trademarks of Berrett-Koehler Publishers, Inc.

Printed in the United States of America.

Berrett-Koehler books are printed on long-lasting acid-free paper. When it is available, we choose paper that has been manufactured by environmentally responsible processes. These may include using trees grown in sustainable forests, incorporating recycled paper, minimizing chlorine in bleaching, or recycling the energy produced at the paper mill.

Library of Congress Cataloging-in-Publication Data

Names: Schein, Edgar H., author. | Schein, Peter A., author.
Title: Humble leadership : the powers of relationships, openness, and trust / Edgar H. Schein, Peter Schein.
Description: First edition. | Oakland, CA : Berrett-Koehler Publishers, Inc., [2018]
Identifiers: LCCN 2018008175 | ISBN 9781523095384 (pbk.)
Subjects: LCSH: Leadership. | Organizational behavior. | Trust.
Classification: LCC HD57.7 .S3428 2018 | DDC 658.4/092—dc23 LC record available at https://lccn.loc.gov/2018008175

First Edition

25 24 23 22 21 | 10 9 8 7 6

Book produced by BookMatters; copyedited by Louise Doucette; proofread by Janet Reed Blake; indexed by Leonard Rosenbaum. Cover design by Susan Malikowski, DesignLeaf Studio

To our grandchildren and their children

Contents

Preface

What This Book Is About

Do you find yourself mired in an individualistic competitive culture of management in which leadership is always about a "superstar" doing something extraordinary and heroic? Would it help to think of leadership *not* as the "seven steps" you must take to lead, but as the energy that is shared in a group that is accomplishing something new and better? This book proposes a relational view of leadership as a process of learning, sharing, and directing new and better things to do in the dynamic interpersonal and group processes that increasingly characterize today's organizations. Such leadership processes can occur at any level, in any team or workgroup, in any meeting, in tight or open networks, in co-located or widely dispersed work units, and across all kinds of cultural boundaries. Leadership can come from group members as often as from designated or appointed leaders. It will rotate unpredictably as the tasks of the groups change in the volatile markets that are changing at an exponential rate.

In our view, leadership is always a *relationship*, and truly successful leadership thrives in a *group culture of high openness and high trust*. Leadership and culture can be seen as two sides of the same coin, and culture is quintessentially a group phenomenon. Though this book focuses on a new model of leadership, it is equally a book about culture and group dynamics.

The traditional twentieth-century culture of management can be described as a transactional set of relationships among designated roles that unwittingly creates conditions of low openness and low trust and can, therefore, make truly effective leadership difficult. We will refer to these transactional relationships as "Level 1," referring to the concept of "levels of relationships" that was first introduced in 2016 in the book *Humble Consulting*. We propose "Humble Leadership" as a model that is intimately tied to a more personal, trusting, and open culture built on more personal intragroup and intergroup relationships. We will refer to this as "Level 2."

We emphasize that the process of leadership can be conceived of as distinct from traditional vertical hierarchy and individual "heroic" performance. *Leading* in business and in the military, *directing* in the arts, *convening* and *organizing* social and political groups, *coaching* professional sports teams, and *founding* new organizations all have in common that such leadership occurs in groups and hinges on open and trusting relationships within those groups. Only Level 2 relationships within those groups enable all members to be inspired to work at their best.

This book is about reasserting that the core of organizational longevity is in the interaction of social, emotional, and cooperative whole human beings in various kinds of personal relationships to each other. Humble leadership can be anything from convening groups to becoming a catalyst that enables them and then disappears until needed again. This model does not displace other models such as servant, or transformative, or inclusive leadership but is, in a sense, the process, the dynamic element that has to be present in any of those models for them to succeed—Humble Leadership concerns itself with creating the culture that makes purposeful forward movement sustainable as the world of work evolves.

Who This Book Is For

This book is for all managers and leaders who have the motivation, the scope, and the flexibility to create change in their organizations. Humble Leadership is most needed in our corporations but is equally relevant to the other sectors of society, such as medicine, the arts, our political institutions, not-for-profits, sports teams, local community organizations, and so on. In fact, we often see archetypes of our model of Humble Leadership in such community organizations, in sports, and in the theater and performance arts.

This model is for leaders, but it is not just for those in leading roles. We assume leadership exists in all corners and levels of all organizations. We see leadership as a complex mosaic of relationships, not as a two-dimensional (top-down) status in a hierarchy, nor as a set of unusual gifts or talents of "high-potential" individuals. This view of leadership should be especially relevant to readers who are in human resources and organization development, because we emphasize that Humble Leadership is as much about the "soft skills" as it is about technology, strategy, authority, discipline, and so on.

We conceive of leadership as more than a role, as a collaborative relationship directed at doing something different, new and better, and it should therefore be relevant to product managers, finance and operations leads, CFOs, board members, investors, doctors, lawyers, and others in the "helping" professions. We hope to find readers at any point in a value chain who can see the impact of designing optimal information-sharing, open, and trusting relationships that improve outcomes by improving the way groups reanimate and reenergize static, role-based organizational designs, and inspire the participants in these groups to give their best *ensemble* performances.

What You Will Gain by Reading This Book

Prescriptive leadership books—and there are many great ones to choose from—offer lists of requisite skills, success formulas, and desirable attributes that will help you climb to the top, to invent the next big thing, to change the world. There is little doubt in our minds that great leadership prescriptions have contributed to the explosive growth in innovation, global expansion, and financial success that characterize the 35 years from the early 1980s to now (early 2018). Our concern is that this focus on heroes and "disrupters" with the right personal values and visions will only go so far in preparing any one of us for the work upheavals we will face in the next 35 years.

What if we proposed that you can reframe the personal challenge of improving your leadership skills into a collective challenge of helping to improve how your groups perform? Consider this book as a way to take the pressure off you to do it all. Instead of heading into work wondering how you alone can solve the problem, what if you went to work committed to sorting it out with a partner, a group, a large or small work team? It's not up to you alone to solve the problem, to lead to greatness, to change the world. It is up to you to create a learning environment in which you and your group can cooperate in identifying and fixing the processes that solve problems, and maybe then change the world. We hope this book gives you some new ways to ask questions, some new ways to learn, in sum, some examples of Humble Leadership that have helped others create change and growth.

Brief Historical Note

We have always been puzzled by this question: "Do leaders create cultures or do cultures create leaders?" We have seen many examples of both and have continued to honor the dichotomy. However, in the last 75 years we have evolved the field of group dynamics and have invented "experiential learning" in group contexts, which has enabled us to observe and manage how group forces (culture) and individual initiative (leading) are in constant interaction. Leaders are constantly shaping cultures, but cultures always limit what defines leadership and what individual change agents will be allowed to get away with. We reaffirmed this point in our fifth edition of *Organizational Culture and Leadership* (Schein & Schein, 2017).

As socialized humans we cannot step outside our culture, but we can begin to understand our culture and see how leadership as a relational activity is both shaped by and shapes culture. We can also begin to see in which direction managerial culture needs to evolve in order to be relevant to the imminent environmental, social, political, economic, and technological changes. The concept of Humble Leadership derives from this need and highlights the interactive nature of leadership as wanting to do something new and better within the boundaries of what the existing culture will accept and, if those boundaries are too restrictive, to begin to change those cultural dimensions.

As the reader will see, the hardest part of this process will be to change elements of the existing managerial culture, which we believe has become ossified if not obsolete. A new model of cooperative leadership may struggle to find its footing in an individualistic competitive transactional culture. So, the first challenge of the emergent humble leader may well be to begin to change that culture.

Conventional managerial culture has never avoided talking about teams and groups as critical (though perhaps not central). Teams still revolve around individuals, as evidenced by team incentives following individual incentives. We still tend to focus incentives on leaders of teams, and yet important research over the last 75 years strongly indicates how *an effective group or team creates the conditions for leadership as much as leaders create effective teams.*

Similarly, transparency and employee engagement are generally espoused, but the degree to which management withholds critical economic information from employees strongly suggests that the culture of management subtly but firmly supports the assumption that management still has the "divine right to tell others what to do" (Schein, 1989).

We concede that Humble Leadership defined as an intrinsically relational process that is deeply embedded in effective group processes, does not displace other models built on individual heroic visions or purposes. Transformational and servant leadership models are highly relevant for today's organizations, but we believe that all these models will require Humble Leadership as a foundational group process. We believe that all modern leadership models can be complemented with a more *personal relational* emphasis if they are to be relevant to an emerging cohort of modern leaders. To this end we introduce the concept *personalization* to highlight the essence of Level 2 Humble Leadership.

How This Book Is Organized

In Chapters 1 and 2 we will describe our vision of Humble Leadership and the relationship theory that serves as the foundation. We will share some stories in Chapters 3, 4, 5, and 6 that illuminate what we see as Humble Leadership success, as well as cases where Humble Leadership did not develop, was stifled, or did not succeed. We will then look ahead in Chapter 7 to highlight some trends we see forcing and reinforcing here-and-now humility, *personization*, group sensemaking, and team learning, all the key components of Humble Leadership. In Chapter 8 we will suggest how Humble Leadership and related group dynamics theory may advance our thinking about broader managerial culture, and in Chapter 9 we will propose what you can do by way of further reading, self-analysis, and skill building to enhance your own Humble Leadership proficiency.

ONE

A New Approach to Leadership

This book introduces a new approach to leadership based more on *personal* relationships than *transactional role* relationships.

The *good* news: employee engagement, empowerment, organizational agility, ambidexterity, innovation... all of this can flourish in the rapidly changing world when the fundamental relationship between leaders and followers, helpers and clients, and providers and customers becomes more personalized and cooperative.

The *bad* news: continued deception, scandals, high turnover of disengaged talent, safety and quality problems in industry and health care, all the way to corruption and abuse of power at the highest levels of industry and politics, driven by financial expediency and the obsession with retaining power as primary success criteria... all of this will continue to happen as long as leader-follower relationships remain impersonal, transactional, and based on the roles and rules that have evolved in the current culture of management that still predominates in our hierarchical bureaucratic organizations.

We therefore need a model of leadership that is more personal and cooperative, that changes relationships both inside organizations and between organization members and their customers, clients, and patients. This model is *Humble Leadership*.

What Is Leadership?
The Leader–Follower Relationship

"Leadership" is wanting to do something *new* and *better*, and getting others to go along. This definition applies as much to senior executives developing new strategies, new purposes, and new values as it does to a group member down in the organization suggesting a new way of running a meeting or improving a process to drive better results. Both the word *new* and the word *better* remind us that leadership always refers to some task that can be improved and to some group whose values and culture will ultimately determine what is better.

What is new and what is better will always depend on context, the nature of the task, and the cultural values that are operating in the group or organization that is doing the work. What we later may label as "good or effective leadership" thus always begins with someone perceiving a new and better way to do something, an emergent leader. Our focus will be not on the individual and the desired characteristics of that emergent leader, but on the relationships that develop between that person and the potential followers who will have influenced what is finally considered to be new and better and who will implement the new way if they agree to try it. Those potential followers will always be some kind of workgroup or team, so our focus will also be on the relationships between them. They may be co-located or widely spread in a network, and their membership may change, but there will always be some kind of grouping involved, hence group dynamics and group processes will always be intimately involved with leadership.

LEVELS OF RELATIONSHIP

Leader-follower relationships can usefully be differentiated along a continuum of "levels of relationship" that are generally accepted in society, that we have learned to use in our own relationships, and that are, therefore, familiar and comfortable. We introduce these levels now but will explain them in greater detail in Chapter 2. The relationship continuum includes these four levels:

- **Level Minus 1**: Total impersonal domination and coercion

- **Level 1**: Transactional role and rule-based supervision, service, and most forms of "professional" helping relationships

- **Level 2**: Personal cooperative, trusting relationships as in friendships and in effective teams

- **Level 3**: Emotionally intimate total mutual commitments

Some version of these levels is present and well understood in most societies, and we generally know the difference in our own relationships between coercively giving orders to someone over whom we have power (Level Minus 1) and the broad range of transactional relationships we have with strangers, service providers, and our bosses, direct reports, and peers with whom we maintain appropriate "professional distance" (Level 1).

These arm's-length relationships differ from how we relate to friends and to teammates in collaborative workgroups we have gotten to know as individual human beings (Level 2), and how we relate to our spouses, close friends, and confidants with whom we share our more intimate and private feelings (Level 3).

We already have the attitudes and skills necessary to decide at what level to relate to each other in our daily lives, but have we thought through sufficiently what is the appropriate level of relationship in our workgroups and in our hierarchical relationships? Have we considered what the leadership relationship needs to be as the tasks of organizations become more complex?

In order to explain what we mean by *Humble Leadership*, we need to consider what these levels mean in the organizational context of today and as we look ahead. Our argument is that Level Minus 1 domination and coercion is a priori morally inappropriate in an established democratic society and is, in any case, ineffective except where tasks are very simple and programmable. Level 1 transactional relationships built around role expectations, and rules of behavior appropriate to those roles, have evolved into what we can think of as the basic managerial culture that still dominates many of our organizations and institutions. It is based on the core US values of individual competitiveness, heroic self-determination, and a concept of work that is linear, machine-like, and based on technical rationality. Level 1, therefore, relies on rules, roles, and the maintenance of appropriate professional distance (Roy, 1970). This existing culture and the way the world is changing lead us to believe that we need a new model based on more personal Level 2, and sometimes even Level 3, relationships and group processes.

Why We Need Another Book about Leadership

There are several reasons why we need a new leadership model.

1. TASK COMPLEXITY IS INCREASING EXPONENTIALLY

The tasks that need to be accomplished in today's world involve a dynamic mix of emerging technologies, collaboration between many kinds of expertise provided by team members, and ecosystem partners, who often come from different occupational and national cultures. The products and services that need to be provided are themselves getting more complex and are constantly shifting in the rapidly changing sociopolitical environment. Information technology and geographically dispersed social networks have created new ways of organizing and communicating, which makes it very hard to define the process of leadership (Heifetz, 1994; Johansen, 2017).

Organizations around the world are struggling with the increasing rate of change, the degree of global interconnectedness, multiculturalism, and the pace of technological advances. Climate change is accelerating. Product specialization is accelerating. Cultural diversification is accelerating. It is becoming obvious that keeping pace in this world will require teamwork and collaboration of all sorts based on the higher levels of trust and openness created by more personalized relationships. Teams will require other teams to share what works and what they know. Humble Leadership at all levels will be needed to link workgroups and teams. Self-centeredness, quid pro quo machinations, political one-upmanship—behaviors that come naturally to individual climbers in hierarchies—will be discredited if not punished as selfish wastes of time.

Organizations who can recast their self-image, design

and redesign themselves to be adaptable living organisms, will increase their own success and survival rate (O'Reilly & Tushman, 2016). This book proposes that this redesign will not happen without more personalized leadership on top of, inside of, and around modern organizations. Humble Leadership will create and reflect the relationships that can respond to this accelerating rate of systemic change and will empower workgroups to build and maintain critical adaptive capacity to capitalize on accelerating change.

A new model is timely. As Frederic Laloux said in his analysis of the evolution of organizational forms, "something is in the air" (Laloux and Appert, 2016, p. 161). We are particularly struck by descriptions of new organization patterns in the US military, America's largest hierarchical organization, which suggest that the only way to fight some of today's wars is with a "team of teams" approach (McChrystal, 2015). Even, or especially, in the US military, the old model—organizations as machines led by heroes—is the past, not the future. It is hard to see how future organizations in most industries will survive if their business model is based primarily on the standardized output machine myth.

Leadership in this environment is categorically *humbling* because it is virtually impossible for an individual to accumulate enough knowledge to figure out all of the answers. Interdependence and constant change become a way of life in which humility in the face of this complexity has become a critical survival skill. For the past 50 years scholars have described the world as an "open socio-technical system" of constantly changing social and business contexts that must be accepted and approached with a "spirit of inquiry." As we move into the future, these conditions will increase exponentially, which will make Humble Leadership a primary means for dealing with these socio-technical challenges.

2. THE CURRENT MANAGERIAL CULTURE IS MYOPIC, HAS BLIND SPOTS, AND IS OFTEN SELF-DEFEATING

We have seen remarkable advances in engineering and in automation that are nearly eliminating technical defects in materials and manufacturing processes. But the design, production, and delivery of a growing number and variety of products has become primarily a socio-technical problem in which the quality and safety issues derive from faulty interactions between the various social micro systems of today's complex organizations.

All too often, problems aren't in the "nodes" (individuals), but in the interactions (relationships). With the exponential rise in contingencies and interactions, we see signs of a deep malaise in many organizations that can be characterized most clearly as the persistent failure of both downward and upward communication, reflecting indifference and mistrust up and down the hierarchy. Quality and safety problems don't result from technological failures but from *socio*-technical failures of communication (Gerstein, 2008).

To make matters worse, the management culture that has worked well so far has also created blind spots and diminished peripheral vision, which prevent many top executives from seeing and taking seriously this communication pathology. We must examine how the very culture that created success so far is built on some values that inhibit new and better ways of doing things.

Downward communication often fails because employees neither understand nor trust what executives declare as the strategy or culture they want to promulgate. Employees often feel that what is asked of them, for example "teamwork and collaboration," is in direct conflict with deeper elements of the culture, such as the *competitive individualism* for which they have been rewarded in climbing the corporate ladder. In our experience, too many top executives are remarkably unwilling or unable to see how their calls for virtuous new cultures of teamwork, of engagement, of becoming more agile and innovative, fall on deaf ears, because they are unwilling to change their own behavior and to build the new reward structures that would be needed to support the new cooperative values.

Upward communication typically fails because employees resist speaking up when they don't understand, don't agree, or see quality and safety issues in how the organization functions (Gerstein, 2008; Gerstein & Schein, 2011). All too often, failure to speak up has led to the deadly accidents that we have seen in the chemical, oil, construction, utility, and even aviation industries. In health care, we have seen hospital-induced infections and unwarranted deaths because employees either did not speak up or were not listened to if they did speak up and/or were told, "Don't worry, it will be taken care of by safety procedures," only to discover later that nothing was done. Complacency and not reporting (false negatives) are often the unseen causes of costly errors.

We have seen in recent scandals involving Volkswagen, Veterans Affairs, and Wells Fargo Bank how unrealistic production and/or cost control targets seemed to ignore employee appeals that they could not meet those targets and led to installing illegal software in cars, lying and falsifying records, or opening thousands of bogus bank accounts. Employee complaints were met in the case of VW with management saying, in effect, "Either you find a way to meet the emission targets with the present engine or we will find others who can!"

When employees occasionally become whistle-blowers,

they may end up being acknowledged and may even effect some change, but all too often at great expense to their own careers (Gerstein, 2008; Schein, 2013b). The management principle "Don't bring me a problem unless you have the solution" is too widely quoted. Even more shocking is when executives tell us that a rise in accident rates and even some deaths is just "the price of doing business." We have heard hospital administrators say something equivalent: "Well, people do die in hospitals!"

Peer-to-peer communication is heavily advocated in all the talk of building teams and better collaboration but is almost always compromised by everyone's recognition that the career reward system is built on competition between individual performers. We talk teamwork, but it is the individual stars who get the big economic rewards and fame. We don't reward groups or hold groups accountable. When things go well, we identify the stars; when things go poorly, we look for someone to blame. We all too often hear of "blame cultures" in organizations. In one such large organization in the oil industry we heard engineers suggest, "When a project is finished, get reassigned immediately so that if anything goes wrong, you won't be around to be blamed!"

Beyond these communication problems we see further issues. We see US business culture continue to espouse the individual *hero* myth leader, and a *machine* model of hierarchical organization design that not only undermines its own goals of employee engagement, empowerment, organizational agility, and innovative capacity, but also limits its capacity to cope with a world that is becoming more volatile, uncertain, complex, and ambiguous (VUCA). Though many managers may deny this, we think the hero model engenders a managerial culture that is implicitly built either on Level Minus 1 coercive relationships or on formal Level 1 hierarchical bureaucratic relationships between managers and employees, which de facto can become coercive and constricting. The leadership model that is generated by this kind of Level 1 managerial culture is dependent on visionary, charismatic leaders to overcome the apathy or resistance that builds up in such transactional, "professionally distant," role-based relationships.

Furthermore, we increasingly see that this form of transactional leading and managing has created not only the organizational communication pathology referred to above, but even what some would call organizational "evil" because employees are seen not as whole human beings, but as roles, commodities, and "resources" (Sennett, 2006; Adams & Balfour, 2009; Gerstein & Schein, 2011; Schein, 2014). In a role- and rule-based organization it is easy to ignore what the safety analysts call "practical drift" (Snook, 2000) or "normalization of deviance" (Vaughan, 1996). Such drift is related to executive myopia, if not tunnel vision, which can allow dysfunctional behaviors to develop throughout the layers of the hierarchy, which, in turn, spawn employee disengagement, lying, cheating, and, ultimately, safety and quality problems for citizens, customers, and patients.

A more extreme example that borders on "evil" was reported in a recent article in the *New Yorker* detailing how a large chicken-producing factory exploits undocumented immigrants, puts them into unsafe environments, and threatens to expose them to deportation if they complain about work conditions (Grabell, 2017). Suffice it to say that we see problems in the existing managerial culture that cannot be fixed by the individual hero models that this same culture advocates.

In defense of the existing culture, as long as leaders understood the task, they could continue to try to impose new and better methods such as Lean or Agile (Shook, 2008). However, as tasks become more socio-technically complex and interdependent, formal leaders often discover that the new and better way is only understood and implemented correctly if employees are actively involved in the design and implementation of those changes, which ultimately hinges on having Level 2 personal relationships in the change groups.

3. THERE ARE GENERATIONAL CHANGES IN SOCIAL AND WORK VALUES

Forces for change in the design of work and organizations are slowly evolving around new social values about what work and organizations should mean in today's complex multicultural world. There is more talk of social responsibility and becoming stewards of our environment and our planet, what is well captured in the idea of "servant leadership" (Greenleaf, 2002; Blanchard, 2003; Blanchard & Broadwell, 2018). New cohorts entering the workforce have different expectations and concepts of what work and career should be. There is a growing emphasis placed on work that is meaningful and based on purpose, work that will enable employees to use their full range of talents and to gain experience for its own sake, not simply for bonuses of money and "things."

So How Is Humble Leadership Different?

To make organizations more effective, to lead what has increasingly come to be labeled "culture change" or "transformation," the relationship between the emergent leader and the organizational followers who will implement the changes has to become a more personal and cooperative Level 2 relationship. We are already seeing a drift toward Level 2 relationships as doctors with patients, product designers with their customers, teachers with their students, and team leaders with their members are discovering that things work better and are emotionally more satisfying when the relationship becomes more personal.

Level 2 personal, open, and trusting relationships have to be developed throughout workgroups to facilitate cultural transformations and build the innovative capacities that the VUCA world will require. Those work relationships may sometimes even drift into varying degrees of Level 3 intimacy, depending on the nature of the task, as in high-stakes operations carried out by military groups such as Navy Seal teams or Army Special Forces, even though Level 3 relationships may still be deemed inappropriate in hierarchical systems such as offices or hospitals.

Various forms of Humble Leadership have existed through-out history when the task required it. Some examples follow.

A Range of Humble Leadership Examples

These examples are actual cases touching on different levels of organizational life. Some are disguised because the organization or the persons did not want to be identified. The common element in the examples is that a humble leader set out to create what we call Level 2 relationships and used implicit knowledge of group dynamics to deal with hierarchy and/or limit the damage of undesirable competitive individualism.

EXAMPLE 1.1. Creating Group Accountability at the Top

A CEO of a large multinational chemical conglomerate
works with an internal board of 11 direct reports and has
made them accountable as a group for the performance of
the organization. They have gotten to know each other at a
personal level through frequent regular meetings in which
basic strategy is discussed and decided.

To enable this joint decision making, they have arranged
to rotate responsibilities for the different product divisions,
international divisions, and functional divisions every 3
years so that each of them will become totally familiar
with all aspects of the business and will never seek to be
an individual champion for any given product, country, or
function.

Their joint accountability creates open dialogues on difficult strategic and operational decisions. They have created
a climate in which no one is afraid to speak up, and they
have conveyed these values to others, especially their direct
reports. Perhaps most important, they have accepted that
learning to function as a group is an especially difficult task
and have used group-oriented process consultants to learn
how to be an effective group. They take time out to review
their group process frequently and discover during those
review periods how leadership has actually been widely
distributed among them. By having each senior executive be familiar with each division, geographical unit, and
function, they avoid destructive self-serving arguments by
representatives.

The example shows that even a highly divisionalized,
multinational organization can create a governance

process in which the "silos" cooperate and are jointly accountable, by building open and trusting relationships between the silos.

EXAMPLE 1.2. Personalizing Hierarchical Relationships

Jerry, a recently retired CEO of a major worldwide manufacturing and services conglomerate, described his managerial and leadership behavior as follows (Seelig, 2017):

> Early in my career I concluded that the success of an organization was critically dependent on the technical competence and leadership skills of those in charge, whatever their title or responsibility within the organization. During my first few months in a new management job, I spent many hours with each and every manager and supervisor discussing their specific operation, asking many questions both about their past performance as well as what each felt were the future opportunities and challenges of the business or activity for which they were responsible. I asked each manager what he or she would do if they had my job and what recommendations they had for me as the new general manager.
>
> I wanted each supervisor and manager to fully understand, and feel comfortable with, my management style. First, I wanted to be told about any significant problems they encountered, but I also expected them to give me their suggestions for solving the problem. Second, I absolutely wanted to listen to their opinion on any issue we discussed. I not only wanted their opinion, I wanted them to argue with me if we disagreed. Only after fully discussing the alternatives and considering the risks

and benefits could we arrive at the most appropriate
solution.

What Jerry described was Humble Leadership in that he
was building personal "helping relationships" (Schein, 2009)
throughout the organization, but especially with direct
and indirect reports. He was openly acknowledging that
he would need the help of his colleagues and reports in
making decisions. He could not understand all the technical work in the different subsidiaries and realized he would
have to work in countries with different cultures. He was
an executive vice president with absolute formal authority
to "run" these units, but how he organized the people below
him reflected his recognition that his job was basically to
build mutual trust and open communication with managers below him. He illustrated through his own behavior
that relationships in a hierarchy did not have to be arbitrary top-down command and control.

EXAMPLE 1.3. Empowering Managers in a Start-Up

The 1950s start-up of Digital Equipment Corp. (DEC)
showed how its founder, as a humble leader, built over 25
years an enormously successful company that was, in size,
second only to IBM. This story also illustrates how Level 2
can be lost and how the "organization as a machine" can
resurface quickly when size and success create internal
conflicts and communication pathologies (Schein, 2003,
2016; Schein & Schein, 2017).

In his role as the cofounder, Ken Olsen hired the best
and brightest young computer engineers he could find,
built personal Level 2 relationships with them, then drafted

them periodically into what he called an "operations committee," took them to 2-day off-sites, posed the key questions about what kinds of products they should develop,
encouraged the unruly debate that invariably resulted,
and more or less withdrew to listen rather than compete
in the debate. He would often physically withdraw, go sit
in the corner of the room, and seem to get lost in his own
thoughts. During the many hours of debate, he would only
come in sporadically with sharp questions, never a suggestion. Only when the group began to achieve some consensus, favoring one proposal that stood up to the criticisms
directed at it, would Ken come back to the table and ask for
a *collective* decision.

Once when Ken was asked why he did not make autocratic decisions, why he let the debate run on and on
sometimes, he quickly countered with, "First of all I am not
that smart. I also learned once, when I made a decision, and
started to walk down the road, I discovered that there was
no one behind me." He realized that making a decision and
getting it implemented required the building of mutual helping relationships that depended on complete openness and
mutual trust. He made it clear that concealing information
from or lying to each other, to him, or even to customers was
absolutely unacceptable and would cause instant dismissal.

Having hired the best technical talent, he accepted his
vulnerability (of not having all the answers as the founder)
but trusted his experts to make the best technical decisions
while he created a personal environment of openness and
trust. He empowered his key employees and made himself
reliant on them. He wanted the *market* to decide whether
the decisions were good ones or not. He humbled himself
both to his employees and to the realities of the market.

Generally speaking, in a new organization it is possible

to empower lower levels to make strategic and tactical decisions. However, if that organization is successful, grows,
and ages, it also begins to experience strong tribalism
because the young engineers who are empowered become,
with age and success, very powerful, build their own
empires, and begin to fight with each other. At DEC, trust
eroded very quickly, leading to many of the pathologies
mentioned above. In the end Ken was increasingly sidelined
by the very people he had empowered.

The DEC board did not have Level 2 relationships with
each other or with Ken, which led to a sad but predictable
outcome. As the tribes fought, they used up limited
resources, leading to three major product releases arriving
late to market. The market had also shifted, and when
DEC could not pivot, Ken was fired and DEC was sold
to Compaq, which eventually was acquired by Hewlett-
Packard. DEC had, however, demonstrated in its first 25
years how a founder could build an organization with
Humble Leadership.

EXAMPLE 1.4. Honoring Safety Over Productivity

Sarah Smith is the head of electrical operations for a large
urban utility. Above her is the vice president of all operations, which includes gas and steam power. This VP is very
concerned about coordination and collaboration between
his various units and therefore has made group meetings
with a facilitator central to his operation. He has mandated
that Sarah should build the same kind of "culture of collaboration" among her four regional managers and asks
her frequently how this is going. He has urged her to use a
group-oriented facilitator to work with her group to ensure

that they build a set of norms that will get them and their reports to speak up if they see any kind of safety or maintenance problem anywhere in the system.

Sarah has learned that only if she spends a lot of time with her direct reports can she count on them to make their reports feel safe in bringing up maintenance problems. She reminds them that safety and reliability are more important than maintaining a schedule, and she rewards any employee who raises maintenance- and safety-related concerns. She is acutely aware that the executives above her really mean it when they say that safety is the highest priority, and they expect her to pass that message on to all the levels below her.

Leaders and managers can reinforce deep values like safety and quality by regularly reminding their direct reports that these values must dominate even if it reduces short-run productivity and compromises timeliness. This message is understood and accepted because Level 2 relationships have been built between the levels.

EXAMPLE 1.5. How a Surgeon Works on Building Trust and Openness

David is the senior spine surgeon in a large urban children's hospital. His complex operations require a team on which he is quite dependent during most of the operation. When asked how he developed a level of trust and openness with his team, he said he first selected people on the basis of their competence and then "took them out to lunch." He realized that the quickest way to reduce the hierarchical distance in the team was to do something very human and nonhierarchical together. He later learned that his wanting to eat with his team rather than with the other doctors also sent an important signal to the team on how important they were. He knew that the quickest way to get to know them as individuals was over an informal activity such as a meal.

Nevertheless, hospital policies changed and he could no longer have a dedicated team, so after that, at the beginning of the operation he encountered strangers who were rotated in to fit the schedule. He still needed to build trust and openness as quickly as possible, so he evolved a process of using the required pre-op checklist in a cooperative way. Instead of hurrying through it as a mechanical matter of course, he asked the chief OR nurse to go through each item slowly and looked at each team member directly, with body language that showed interest and readiness to hear questions or issues about each item from each person. He made it very clear how important their contributions were and tried to convey the message that they must work together and must totally trust each other. Trust in this context was visually and physically developed in near-real time, by the simple if not symbolic task of the group reviewing the checklist.

This story highlights that if a team clearly shares a common goal, personal relationships can be built very quickly if the leader desires and chooses to build on existing structure and conventions to facilitate a cooperative process.

The Implications of What We Are Arguing

Organizations today are doing all kinds of experiments in how work is defined and are showing great flexibility in how roles and authority are allocated. What we see in these experiments is that they encourage relationships that are more personal. Bosses, direct reports, team members, and resources from other teams are making it a point to get to know each other at a more personal level, fostering more openness and, in time, more trust and the psychological safety to speak up and be heard.

In a Level 2 relationship, I convey that "I see you." This is not necessarily "I like you," or "I want to be your friend," or "Let's get our families together," but I let you know through my words, demeanor, and body language that I am aware of your total presence, that in this relationship we are working together and are dependent on each other, are trying to trust each other, and should each try to see each other as more than a fellow employee, or associate, or team member, but as a whole person. Seeing each other as whole persons is primarily a choice that we can make. We already know how to be personal in our social and private lives. Humble Leadership involves making that conscious choice in our work lives. To summarize,

- Humble Leadership builds on Level 2 personal relationships that depend on and foster openness and trust.

- If Level 2 relationships do not already exist in the workgroup, the emergent humble leader's first job is to develop trust and openness in the workgroup.

- In a Level 2 workgroup Humble Leadership emerges by enabling whoever has pertinent information or expertise to speak up and improve whatever the group is seeking to accomplish.

- The process of creating and maintaining Level 2 relationships requires a learning mindset, cooperative attitudes, and skills in interpersonal and group dynamics.

- An effective group dealing with complex tasks in a volatile environment will need to evolve such mindsets, attitudes, and skills in all of its members.

- Therefore, Humble Leadership is as much a group phenomenon as an individual behavior.

Summary and Plan of Action

We have described the concept of *level of relationship* as the basis for defining what we mean by Humble Leadership. We have also argued that the historically derived current culture of management, built on a number of deep assumptions about employees as role occupants, as "human resources," cannot see how its own values and assumptions create some of the quality, safety, and employee engagement problems that we see today. A new model built on different assumptions is therefore needed.

These new assumptions are based on the fundamental proposition that we need to build not on individual competencies, but on models of relationships and group dynamic processes. Understanding Humble Leadership hinges on understanding levels of relationships, which is the focus of the next chapter.

> The future needs a new concept,
> **Humble Leadership**,
> which is built on **Level 2**
> relationships of openness and trust.

TWO

Culturally Defined Levels of Relationship

All leadership theories acknowledge that leadership involves "relationships," yet very few take the trouble to analyze and explain what they mean by that word. For us, the concept of relationship refers sociologically to how people connect with each other. When we discuss managerial culture, we will argue that these interpersonal connections have a particular meaning in the context of hierarchy and bureaucracy. Inasmuch as we are focusing on different *levels* of relationship, we must begin by explaining what we mean by the word itself and by showing how the US cultural context provides implicitly defined relationship levels around which we can build our particular work-related Level 2 concept. To fully understand the process of Humble Leadership, it is necessary to understand the subtle interactions that occur in a relationship and how these relate to levels of openness and trust.

What Is a Relationship?

A relationship is a set of *mutual expectations* about each other's future behavior based on past interactions with one another. We have a relationship when we can anticipate each other's behavior to some degree. When we say we have a "good relationship," this means that we feel a certain level of comfort with the other person, comfort that is based on this sense of knowing how the other will react. Further, we share confidence that we are both working toward a goal that we have agreed upon or take for granted. That feeling of comfort is often what we mean by the word *trust*. We "know" what to expect of each other. Our level of trust reflects the degree to which our behavior and the behavior of the other are consistent.

Relationship is by definition an interactive concept. For a relationship to exist, there must be some symmetry in mutual expectations. If I trust you but you don't trust me, then by definition we don't have a trusting relationship. If I can anticipate your behavior but you cannot anticipate mine, then a relationship has not yet formed. If I love you but you don't love me, we may still have a formal transactional relationship, but it is asymmetrical and will likely either progress or end. Symmetry is built within a given culture by what we are taught to expect of each other in the normal social roles we acquire. We know what to expect around gender, around hierarchical relationships, and in the role-based transactions that make up our daily routines. We are taught how to react to each other in these role relations. We call this good manners, civility, and tact.

These learned and prescribed interactive conversational routines are taught to us as we mature. We also learn how much we can trust each other and how open we can be with each other in the many different situations we may face. The degree to which I can trust you, the degree to which you will be open with me, and will respect what I tell you, is prescribed in our culture by the roles we play in our daily transactions. Implicit in those roles is the prescription of how open and how trusting we are supposed to be. If we ask for directions, we expect a truthful response. If we are buying a used car off a lot, we may expect a less truthful conversation. What is often forgotten, however, is that the rules governing civility and tact differ in the different levels of relationship. Let's look again at the four levels we are defining and then examine the implications in terms of what we mean when we say that Humble Leadership has to operate at Level 2.

Four Levels of Relationships

Level Minus 1: Total impersonal domination and coercion

Level 1: Transactional role and rule-based supervision, service, and most forms of "professional" helping relationships

Level 2: Personal cooperative, trusting relationships as in friendships and in effective teams

Level 3: Emotionally intimate total mutual commitments

Degree of *Personization* as the Critical Differentiator of Levels

Personization is not a typo but the introduction of a new concept to clarify what is the ultimate difference between the levels and to differentiate this concept from "personalization," which has come to be associated with customization, the process of offering services or products to people on the basis of their personal choices or needs.

Personization is the process of mutually building a working relationship with a fellow employee, teammate, boss, subordinate, or colleague based on trying to see that person as a whole, not just in the role that he or she may occupy at the moment. *Personization* begins to occur when either party, early in the conversation, asks something personal or reveals something personal. *Personization* implies that one or both parties in the conversation have invested themselves to a considerable degree and have made themselves vulnerable to being ignored or dismissed or disrespected. In all interactions, we invest something and expect something in return. *Personization* is intrinsically a reciprocal interactive process.

Why would you as a manager want to *personize* your relationship with your direct reports? Why would you as an employee want to *personize* your relationship with your boss? Our basic argument is that you would want to do this in order to maximize the possibility that you will be open and honest with each other and will feel safe in reporting when things are not going well, when you don't understand each other, when you don't agree with each other, and, most important, when you need each other's help. You will want to build this relationship in order to be able to trust that your direct reports or peers or your own boss will make commitments in the service of shared goals and will deliver on whatever promises have been made. In building this relationship, you will also want your direct reports or peers or boss to begin to feel that they can trust you to be open and honest with them.

Personizing has nothing to do with being nice, giving employees good jobs and working conditions, generous benefits, or flexible working hours. It has everything to do with building relationships that get the job done and that avoid the indifference, manipulation, or, worse, lying and concealing that so often arise in work relationships.

In the interactions that occur between you and your direct reports, you will minimize "subordination" in order to emphasize collaboration, joint responsibility, and your own willingness to help *them* to succeed. Moving to Level 2 is expressing, in actions and words, "I want to get to know you better so that we can trust each other in getting our jobs done better." We don't need to become friends and learn all about each other's private lives, but we have to learn to be open and honest around work issues.

We believe that it is possible to have a closer, more open and trusting relationship in the work situation while being quite sensitive to boundaries of privacy and propriety. We can know each other well enough at work to trust each other and get the job done without necessarily becoming friends or doing things together outside of work. At the same time, if the work demands a higher level of collaboration (as might be typified by a team of Navy Seals), we can build more re-flexive or intimate relationships as needed to support the higher level of trust and communication that extreme cir-cumstances may demand.

In summary, it is crucial to understand this *personizing* process because it is ultimately the mechanism by which the level of trust that we need in interdependent work situations is built. We need to understand that there is some trust in each level but for Humble Leadership we need a level of trust that is most closely associated with Level 2 relationships. Let's look at each level from the point of view of how *person-ization* influences openness and trust, especially how Level 1 managerial culture has evolved in a way that undermines openness and trust.

Level Minus 1: Negative Relationships

This level pertains only to the unusual situation where we basically do not treat one another as human at all, as might be the case between "master" and slaves, a prison guard and prisoners, or, sadly, some caretakers and emotionally sick or elderly patients at a hospital or nursing home. In the organizational world, we would rarely expect to find such exploitation or indifference, but we occasionally see it in sweatshops, in the factories of some other countries, and, unfortunately, in the attitudes of some managers who view their employees as merely hired hands. Where Level Minus 1 is accepted, employees typically characterize their work situation as "inhuman" but tolerate it because they feel they have no choice. For example, we referred earlier to the recent *New Yorker* article (Grabell, 2017) that describes in some detail how a major producer of chicken exploits undocumented immigrants by reporting them to the authorities for deportation if they complain about low wages, long hours, or unsafe or inhuman working conditions.

Personization is absent in this relationship, which makes organizational "leadership" impossible because the potential followers will neither understand nor be motivated to do what the appointed leader may want them to do. But, as we know, some prisoners will accept a Level 1 transactional relationship with their captors by becoming "trusties" or collaborators, while most will hunker down into apathy or form more personal Level 2 relationships among themselves. For example, in the Chinese and North Korean POW camps during officially sanctioned outings on rafts to get some fresh air on the river, the prisoners organized the following routine: one person would "accidentally" fall overboard, forcing the guards to rush over to rescue him, only to discover, just as they had safely pulled him on board, that another POW had fallen off the other side of the raft, with everyone putting on "innocent" faces (Schein, 1956). Inventing these new ways to harass the guards and to amuse themselves became an important distributed Level 2 leadership process among the POWs.

Domination and coercion by officials results first in creating closer Level 2 relationships among the dominated, and then to inventive ways to defeat the purpose of the officials, which in industrial/plant situations becomes one of the forces leading to unionization. Paradoxically and, in a sense, tragically, what begins as an effective counter-organization subculture may itself develop hierarchy and formal bureaucracy, which can result in far less effective leadership within the union and more explicit intergroup conflict between "management and labor."

Level 1: Transactional, Bureaucratic, and "Professional" Relationships

As members of civilized society, we expect, at the minimum, to *acknowledge* each other as fellow human beings. We expect others to notice our presence even if we don't "know" each other except in our assigned jobs or roles. Level 1 relationships are acknowledged to be impersonal and dispassionate except when something unexpected happens that arouses anxiety or anger, such as being bumped into or threatened or in some other way "disrespected." Interactions or conversations are highly routinized exchanges of give-and-take based on mutual expectations and low levels of personal investment. I give you something, you say thank you; you ask me a question, I feel obligated to answer. This is so automatic that we notice it only when it breaks down, when someone is not civil, or when someone gets "too personal."

Level 1 relationships cover a wide range including how we deal with strangers or casual acquaintances; how we deal with our bosses, peers, and direct reports at work; and how we manage the very personal service connections we have with doctors, lawyers, and other experts upon whom we rely. Level 1 relationships are common in the daily routines of life, punctuated from time to time with more personal Level 2 connections. What distinguishes these routine relationships is that the linkage is between two *roles*, symbolized best by the reality that when we go to a hospital or clinic, we may meet different doctors every time even for the same complaint, or at work we may have new bosses after reorganizations. In these various exchanges we may be personally uncomfortable about seeing different people in the same role, but from society's point of view, this should be acceptable because the persons in the roles are assumed to have equivalent competence in whatever the roles require. We treat each other as fellow humans whom we trust to a certain degree not to harm us and with whom we have polite levels of openness in conversation, but we do not feel the need to "know" each other except in our various roles and statuses.

Much of our work life occurs at Level 1 because the services, stores, hospitals, and businesses we deal with are organized bureaucratically to deal with us at that level. This is typically the source of our dissatisfaction with bureaucracies. We don't like being treated so impersonally, especially at work. And we especially don't like it when our bosses put on a show of being personal but we sense that they do it because they were told that this is desirable, that getting their employees involved or engaged is important. We can usually see right through it, and this can make us indifferent if not resentful. In other words, *the leader cannot fake a Level 2 relationship*. Humans have a very good sense for authenticity, sincerity, and consistency especially when we see these as critical for work relationships.

In routine Level 1 conversations the norm or rule is to uphold and not to upset the "social fabric." This is made possible by the common understanding that the connection is formal and distant and does not require or tolerate much personal investment. Consider the "bystander syndrome," wherein a person is willing to observe but not willing to get involved in situations that would require more personal investment. But even at this level we play by the rules of reciprocation that the culture demands. For example, when someone announces, "Let me tell you something funny I heard the other day," it is almost certain that no matter how unfunny the story or joke is, the others will provide some form of laughter to compensate for the effort to amuse.

The concept of "face" refers to this required mutual support. Face can be thought of as the amount of value we claim in any given situation. In normal Level 1 social interaction we try to maintain each other's face, by which we mean we do not want to devalue what is conversationally offered to us. We laugh at the joke, we respond to questions, and we try to adopt a role comparable to the other person's projected role and level of emotional investment. We each play the role of a responsible adult maintaining good rapport.

If we are trying to enhance the relationship, we respond by adding value through positive responses, praise, acknowledgment, or an equivalently high-value comment such as a complementary joke or a more personal comment. We may say, "That was a great joke" or "I really appreciated that." If we want to curtail the relationship, we can actually be rude and say, "I did not find that very funny," or we can play one-upmanship and say, "I heard a better one than that…." If we are seriously trying to get to know the other person better, we *personize* by asking more personal questions or revealing something more personal about ourselves.

THE LIMITATIONS OF ROLE-RELATED TRUST
AND OPENNESS

Even with the psychological and social distance that we experience with strangers, some level of trust and openness is expected and taken for granted. Most of us have internalized the cultural rules of civility, good manners, tact, and political correctness that make social activities and exchanges possible. We expect a great deal from each other in our various transactional relations when we need services of various kinds, when we engage in the bureaucratic relationships of organizational life, and, most relevant to this analysis, in the role-related transactions that we call "professional."

Under normal conditions we expect to tell each other the truth, but we have also learned that if we think that telling the truth will be hurtful to the other person, or will put one of us at a disadvantage, it is acceptable to withhold or even to lie. In a sales relationship we expect a certain amount of exaggeration and spinning, and in developing social relationships we expect a certain amount of flattering and mutual support. In many sales and service transactions we are intrinsically on guard, hence the term *caveat emptor* (buyer beware). With professional helpers we seek recommendations, and we hope not to be cheated, lied to, or tricked.

Level 1 relationships assume social or professional distance. The concept of professional distance is especially relevant in doctor-patient or lawyer-client relationships where the doctor or lawyer is a specialist who is expected to know more and deliver both diagnosis and prescription. This legitimizes the expert's asking the client all kinds of personal questions. At the same time, it is accepted that the patient or client cannot legitimately ask such questions of the doctor or lawyer in return.

It is assumed that it is in the patient's interest to be truthful and trusting, yet there is growing evidence that, for various reasons, patients withhold information or fail to tell doctors when they are not following their treatment prescriptions (Gawande, 2014). Unfortunately, this often compromises the shared goal of improving health. Similarly, clients often withhold information from their lawyers, which compromises the quality of the legal help that they get. It is common for direct reports not to tell the boss all of the troubles they are having implementing what the boss wants. If asked directly how things are going, an employee may find it easier to respond with obfuscation, "Fine, no problems, everything is under control," even when it is not. The employee may not want to be "the messenger who is shot," may wish to help the boss "save face," or may have learned over time that the boss does not want to hear bad news anyway.

Consider this example: an orthopedic surgeon who is doing a straightforward operation to fix a broken bone can probably depend on the anesthesiologist, the OR nurse, and other members of the team to provide reliable information as the operation proceeds. We have heard doctors assert that it is the "professional responsibility" of the team members to speak up. Unfortunately, we have also heard many younger doctors and nurses admit that they did not dare speak up to the senior surgeon.

On the other hand, as our Example 1.5 showed, a surgeon who is doing a complex and delicate spine operation, confronted in the operating room with a team of strangers, will realize that just depending on the "professional competence" and goodwill of the team members will not guarantee open communication and collaboration. He or she will, therefore, need to make a special effort, like a deep dive with the checklist, to signal a feeling of dependency on them. This is in essence an immediate here-and-now attempt to *per-*

sonize, to get past the role relationships and build a more personal Level 2 relationship in order to increase the likelihood that any member of the ad hoc team will speak up if something needs attention or if it seems the surgeon is about to make a mistake.

In summary, Level 1 relationships based on our various roles are the bulk of our daily routines. If the work we do is programmed enough, these relationships can work smoothly. Our argument that we need to move to Level 2 is based on the observation that the nature of work itself is changing rapidly in a direction that requires more *personized* relationships that create psychological safety and, thereby, increase communication, collaboration, and mutual help.

Level 2: Relationships That Acknowledge the Whole Person

The paradox of Level 2 is that we know how to function at this level with friends and family but often do not choose to do so at work, because we find it neither safe nor rewarding.

The essence of Level 2 is that the other person, whether boss, employee, peer, or partner, moves from being seen as a "role"—a partial or undifferentiated person who must be kept "professionally distant"—to being seen as a *whole* person with whom we can develop a more personal relationship around shared goals and experiences. Level 2 covers all forms of friendship and close acquaintanceship, but for the purpose of evolving the managerial culture, we want to limit Level 2 to work relationships. Within this boundary, we propose that managers, doctors, lawyers, and other helping professionals can begin to build a more personal relationship with their direct reports, patients, and clients, from the very first contact. By opening the door to *personization* at the outset, both parties can begin to treat each other as whole persons rather than roles. They can begin "to see" each other (Schein, 2016). *Personization* can happen very rapidly if we choose to ask something personal or reveal something personal about ourselves. For example, an employee may notice a photo of the boss in foul weather gear and ask, "Are you a sailor?" or notice a family picture and ask, "Is this your family?" and thereby immediately invite a more personal conversation.

As a manager, if you *personize,* you will minimize "subordination" in order to emphasize collaboration, joint responsibility, and your own willingness to help your direct reports to succeed. Moving to Level 2 is expressing, in actions and words, "I want to get to know you better so that we can trust each other in getting our jobs done better." We don't need to become friends and learn all about each other's private lives, but we have to learn to be open and honest around work issues.

This kind of relationship implies a deeper level of trust and openness in terms of (1) making and honoring commitments and promises to each other, (2) agreeing to not undermine each other or harm what we have agreed to do, and (3) agreeing not to lie to each other or withhold information relevant to our task.

We believe that it is possible to have a closer, more open and trusting relationship in the work context while being quite sensitive to boundaries of privacy and propriety. We can know each other well enough at work to trust each other and get the job done without necessarily becoming friends or doing things together outside of work.

A Level 2 work relationship will not be automatic just because the boss or employee wants it to be. Relationships are developed and negotiated through many interactions in which *personizing* efforts are made and responded to and succeed or fail. In the above example, the boss may respond enthusiastically or dismissively to the question about sailing, thereby sending a signal about his or her desire to *personize*. Level 2 is built gradually with experiments in openness that reveal to each party what the limits of comfort are and where there is a threat of going too far into private matters.

As Amy Edmondson has pointed out in her influential work on "teaming" (Edmondson, 2012), *learning together* is one of the best ways to "get to know each other," because in that context the boss and the employee can give each other direct feedback and suggestions on how the work could be done better. This does not mean that they necessarily become friends but that they know each other's whole person in the context of getting the job done; they get to know accurately their skill sets and those aspects of personality that bear on the task to be done.

Edmondson provides a potent example in her study of surgical teams trying a new and difficult operation. The teams who tried it and abandoned it as being "too complicated" relied on individual professional skill; the teams who were able to use the procedures had first been assembled by the cardiac surgeon after a request for commitment and had then made a joint decision to engage in a period of mutual learning with simulations that led to increased trust and openness (Edmondson et al., 2001). The surgeon in Example 1.5 was trying to achieve this rapidly by emphasizing a carefully shared review of the checklist.

There is today a great deal of emphasis on "engaging" employees, giving them time for personal projects, engaging their talents more systematically. However, one can only engage a person, not a role. The manager who is concerned about employee engagement, involvement, and empowerment should focus on creating Level 2 relationships first.

To summarize, we believe that the level of a work relationship should ultimately reflect the nature of the work to be
done. The more the work requires collaboration, open communication, and trust in each other's commitment, the more
it will require Level 2 *personized* relationships. There will
continue to be types of work for which Level 1 transactional
relationships will suffice. But we need to be clear that those
relationships have limitations around openness and trust
that cannot be fixed just by asserting that there will be more
openness and trust. *Evolving the managerial culture from
Level 1 to Level 2 is the defining task for Humble Leadership.*

Level 3: Intimacy and Emotional Attachment, Friendship, and Love

Level 3 relationships are what we might call "intimate" or
"close," friendships that go beyond the more casual Level 2
connections. This level is more emotionally charged and
implies all of the trust and openness of Level 2 but, in addition, assumes that we will actively support each other
as needed and actively display emotional, loving behavior
toward each other. Level 2 implies support and avoiding
harming each other. Level 3 implies actively seeking ways of
helping and enhancing each other.

We deepen our relationship through successive cycles of
revealing more and more of our personal, even private feelings, reactions, and observations, and we calibrate others'
levels of acceptance of what we are revealing by their reciprocation with their own revelations. Successive levels of rev-
elation and reciprocal acceptance ultimately lead to a level
of intimacy in which all parties are comfortable, and this
level will vary with personality and situation. *Personization*
itself will vary in level: In very close relationships we monitor

how personal we should be, both in terms of protecting each other's face and in terms of recognizing personal boundaries, which we all have even within Level 3 relationships. In work relationships it will also vary with the task.

It is generally assumed that we want to avoid Level 3 in organizational life because it can become fraternization, nepotism, and inappropriate favoritism, each of which is considered in managerial culture to be an impediment to getting work done, if not outright corrupt. Bosses are not supposed to get involved in the personal lives of their own bosses, peers, or direct reports. Office romances are generally considered inappropriate, especially when no attempt is made to conceal the intimacy. Gifts and payoffs are not considered legitimate as incentives to get things done. These and other norms of appropriate and inappropriate exchange apply to all working relationships.

The distinction between Level 2 and Level 3 is essentially a matter of degree, and the boundary may vary as a function of the task. This is why it is so tricky in the work setting—we reveal something more intimate about ourselves or ask more personal intimate questions of each other to test whether they are well received or offensive and thereby learn what level of intimacy feels comfortable and is relevant to getting the work done. Over the past few years we have observed US work culture appearing to explore this boundary, as indicated by our use of the colloquial "TMI," or too much information, a constructive signal that perhaps the level of personal information shared is just over the threshold of appropriateness. For some of us such personal questions, responses, and revelations are parts of an easy natural process; for others of us they are awkward. We all know how to *personize* in various settings, so the issue becomes one of legitimizing such conversations in the workplace, even if they feel difficult or untoward, because it is important to getting the work done safely and completely.

It is inescapable that the boundaries between Level 2 and Level 3 will be situational, individual, shared, and dynamic. Our culture provides guidelines and limits for openness and intimacy, and each of us builds up a personal sense of what is private, to be shared only with exceptionally close friends and family members. Yet it is always contextual. There are some remarkable outliers, tasks and situations such as those involving high-performance teams, where we might assume that Level 1 professionalism is the norm, but success in fact demands relationships much more akin to Level 3. In these cases, several of which are described in Chapter 5, successful completion of the mission requires a high level of intimate knowledge of how each person works, an extreme physical form of "finishing the other person's sentences," or an almost extrasensory cooperation based on, at the risk of introducing another term, "super-empathy."

In defining these levels, we are not asserting that the boundaries are initially clear or that the responses of others are always predictable. Part of building the Level 2 relationship is to mutually discover the boundaries of *personization* as each party calibrates how the other responds to a change in degree of openness and finds the level of comfort where both trust each other and can count on each other to be persistently open and truthful.

We have to underscore this last point—Level 2 is *not* about being nice or getting to like each other, though that may be an incidental benefit or may make it easier to achieve the goal. In workgroups Level 2 is critical, however, to provide each member psychological safety, to open bi-directional communication, build trust, and, thereby, accomplish the task faster if not better.

Summary and Conclusions

We have defined what a relationship is and have argued that we consciously or unconsciously create relationships through the various sequences of behavior that we exhibit in different situations. In that sense, relationships can be *designed and evolved*, and the design process begins in the very first interaction between any two people, or within a group, or when a supervisor and a new employee first meet each other.

We have discussed four levels of relationship marked by different degrees of trust and openness based on different degrees of *personization*. The definitions of the four levels are fairly clear at the extremes, but when we are defining "working relationships," we have to acknowledge that within Level 1 there can be fairly open and trusting relationships based on clear task and role definitions, and in Level 2 there is a wide range of degrees of *personizing* depending on the task.

The challenge for Humble Leadership is to build Level 2 trust and openness by becoming more personal, either in what is asked about or in what is revealed, while, at the same time, avoiding both the formality of Level 1 professional distance and the violations of privacy that might be perceived as Level 3 intimacy. A defining skill of Humble Leadership is the ability to manage this balance between being too formal at one extreme and being too intimate at the other extreme.

> Transactional, role-based
> relationships need to become
> *personized*, Level 2 relationships.

THREE

Humble Leadership in Governance: The Singapore Story

That Singapore is offered here as a prime example of Humble Leadership may strike the reader as odd in that Singapore is often presented as an example of authoritarian dictatorship. Dictatorship and Humble Leadership seem categorically incompatible. However, the approach that the early leaders Lee Kuan Yew, Goh Keng Swee, and their colleagues took to building a modern city-state out of an economically declining colony illustrates two important points: first, that Humble Leadership does not mean soft or nice and, second, that Humble Leadership can be passed down through the organization to become a Level 2 culture throughout the government and the key economic institutions it creates. We believe Humble Leadership contributed to Singapore's economic success!

This summary and analysis is based on observations and interviews that Ed and his wife Mary did on the culture of Singapore's Economic Development Board from 1993 to 1995, and on various visits with Singaporeans over the last several decades, most recently with Philip Yeo during his visit to Stanford in 2017 (Schein, 1996; Schein & Schein, 2017).

Historical Summary

The Singapore story is a clear case of Humble Leadership because Lee and his colleagues had very strong Level 2 relationships based on their getting to know each other when they were students in the UK in the 1940s. They knew that their job as future leaders would be incredibly complicated and ambitious yet needed to be tackled with a series of both long-range strategic goals and short-run pragmatic moves.

They recognized that they had a complex socio-technical problem in that their economic survival depended on getting major companies to invest in Singapore, which would not be possible if Singapore did not create an environment that would be attractive and reassuring to skeptical foreign investors. Simply, it meant "cleaning up" the city, changing many elements of the citizens' behaviors, and creating a completely noncorrupt government.

The most difficult part of a long-range strategy of attracting foreign investment and convincing corporations to build plants and research centers in Singapore was to create an absolutely trustworthy corruption-free government that could make and keep commitments. In interviews of CEOs that invested in Singapore, the first thing they said as the reason for such investment was that "there was absolutely no corruption and they kept their promises" (Schein, 1996).

To make Singapore attractive to foreign executives, Lee and his "team" created draconian rules to make the city squeaky clean and to build an airport so pristine that visitors noted, "This reminds me of the Zürich airport." To make these dictatorial policies palatable to the citizenry, Lee made it clear that those policies were based on a strategy of economic development that would give everyone a job and a home, and he backed up these policies with immediate implementation on both fronts.

The economic plan would be administered by creating in 1961 an economic development board (EDB), which was a quasi-governmental organization populated by some of the very best executives Singapore had available, such as Philip Yeo, who became its first chief executive. Everyone in the government had multiple jobs, and teamwork became a central value built around the shared purpose of building Singapore. This required all members in the government to foster a high degree of openness, trust, and collaboration. One mechanism to ensure such collaboration was for some of the senior leaders to have multiple jobs and to rotate them frequently to ensure familiarity with all the elements of government. Job rotation, as in Example 1.1, reinforced "group accountability," which supplemented individual accountability in an important way, stimulating mutual cooperation across the units that, in other systems, often end up competing with each other.

To create a government that could work in this open and trusting way with foreign investors, Lee had recruited the best and brightest young Singaporeans, given them excellent scholarships to go to the best overseas universities, then brought them back for 5 years of service in the government at competitive pay levels.

Humble Leadership showed up in this context in several different ways. First of all, Lee and his associates sought the help of the United Nations and various European advisers who might have had comparable experiences of building a young country. Lee knew what he did not know, and he was not afraid to ask for help. As various industries located themselves in Singapore, government officials were quick to learn from industry how best to run certain things. When interviewed by Ed in 1994, Lee pulled out with great pride a set of manuals for personnel administration, which he had mandated for use in his government. He said that he chose these manuals because the Royal Dutch Shell Company, an organization that he admired very much, used them.

The organization of the EDB illustrated how hierarchy and bureaucracy do not automatically lead to the problems that we mentioned in Chapters 1 and 2. Rather, if the principle is to build open and trusting relationships, that is, Level 2 relationships, it is possible to have both a strict hierarchy and clear roles as long as a high value is placed on everyone's knowing everyone else at an appropriately personal level and on sharing a common overall goal.

Officers of the EDB had both the license and the mandate to talk to anyone up or down the hierarchy if it involved information about present or future investors. Promotions were clearly based on a combination of individual talents and demonstrated ability to collaborate with others. Frequent job rotations through multiple jobs made it possible for everyone to get to know everyone else so that trust and openness could be maintained. In interviews of young EDB officers, they routinely said that they were in competition with each other for promotion but that the ability to form and work in teams was one of the main criteria on which they were competitively evaluated.

The EDB became an international organization with officers placed in all the major industrial centers to develop connections that might lead to investment in Singapore. It was striking how well educated and knowledgeable EDB officers were technically and how well trained they were in the interpersonal skills needed to do their work. Communications to headquarters and to each other were frequent and completely open. On paper, the EDB was a traditional hierarchy and bureaucracy, but it was able to function like an interconnected team, with high trust based on open communications making this possible.

Lee was clearly in charge and was perceived by most of the world as a strong dictator, leading to strong critiques of his suppression of dissenting political parties that would undermine his long-range strategy. He justified this by delivering on his promises to give people jobs and housing. He groomed his son to take over eventually, which, of course, brought up the negative image of nepotism. At the same time, it was clear that the son would have to demonstrate all the talents needed to continue to promote Singapore's growth. It is not nepotism per se that is a flaw in theories of organization design, but the promotion of relatives without the requisite managerial talent. Singapore's government was so open that the son's absence of talent not only would have been visible, but would have made his rise impossible.

An Unforeseen Confirmation

Singapore's success is by now well known, and the Level 2 culture in the government that was established and thrives today was recently confirmed for us by a visit from Philip Yeo. He had maintained his relationship with Ed over the years, was visiting Stanford, and invited Peter and Ed to a meeting in a biotech research lab on campus.

Philip had moved from being the head of the EDB, through various other government jobs, such as running the defense department and building the biotech sector. That meant recruiting and forming partnerships with biotech companies that would do some of their research and production in Singapore. Philip had acquired such a company in Germany in 2016 and was developing research connections with selected Stanford professors.

Philip and Ed had become friends during the EDB research project, so Philip wanted to visit with Ed, meet Peter, and introduce us to the leaders of the German company Singapore was partnering with. It was striking to us how informal this meeting was, how open Philip was with us and with his two biotech executives, the German CEO, and the American COO. Considering that there were three rank levels, three cultures, and two outsiders in this meeting, it was truly remarkable how candid and trusting our conversation was for over an hour on all aspects of what was happening in this new company, in Singapore, and in the world.

What we saw in Philip was a driven, entrepreneurial, fast-moving executive who clearly was able to *personize* and, thereby, quickly establish Level 2 relationships with executives in his management teams. All of this comes through in the interview quotes that appeared in a recent biography written about Philip Yeo by Peh Shing Huei (2016), in which Yeo describes himself as a salesman, a hustler, a go-getter, and one who asks the question "Why not?" rather than "Why?" We emphasize this to suggest strongly that there is nothing incompatible between Level 2 *personization* and all the other dynamic qualities that are associated with great leaders and entrepreneurs.

Peh interviewed many of Philip's colleagues who called themselves "Mad Cows" for "Making A Difference, Changing Our World." They described Yeo's leadership style as "kite-flying" leadership:

> To get the best out of people, don't be paternalistic. You
> have to treat them like kites. . . . You get them up in the air, if
> there's no wind you try again. Everybody needs a lift off. If
> they get into trouble, you reel them in. (Peh, 2016, p. 204)

Yeo detested micromanagement. He let the kites fly. Is this a unique case of an unusual individual with unusual talents? Perhaps, though Ed met many such people when he did his research in the mid-1990s, and in the biography Yeo repeatedly makes the point that his entrepreneurial activities were strongly supported by Goh, his boss, who often went out on a limb to defend decisions that were highly controversial. What made this possible was the absolute trust between Lee, Goh, and Yeo based on their really "knowing each other" and Yeo's getting to know the people he recruited and counted on in his recent acquisitions.

So far it appears that Singapore has been able to maintain their Level 2 culture and resist the regression to Level 1 polarization (in silos) and its attendant loss of openness and trust. As we reflect on this story, it becomes clear that Level 2 relationships had to be present in the founders and subsequent leaders and that they collectively recognized how important it was to maintain such relationships during their successful growth. This hinged very much on the processes of locating the best and brightest, providing a good education for them, employing them in the civil service at levels comparable to business, and strongly reinforcing the value of cooperation in the service of the overall strategic goal.

THE EVOLUTION OF ROLES AND RELATIONSHIPS: GROWTH AND HUBRIS

If the leaders of the governance process have Level 2 relationships with each other, they can create cultural norms that support high openness and high trust within a hierarchical organization. This can be accomplished by not letting roles become rigid and by frequent rotation of key people through key roles so that each knows what is involved in the others' jobs.

Again, we suggest that Humble Leadership is a process, reflecting not character traits as much as collective values that groups bring to their work. In small start-ups and single-focus companies, maintaining openness and trust may be so vital that it is as normal, natural, and life sustaining as breathing. However, with age, success, growth, and new generations of leaders (as was the case with DEC in example 1.3 on page 15), Humble Leadership may become vulnerable to its own success.

Here we believe a real risk associated with increased organizational scale is regression to Level 1 transactional leadership, creating "professional distance," thereby not seeing new and better ways to do things, or not developing Level 2 relationships with the right people to lead in a new direction. One related vulnerability is cronyism and nepotism, wherein chosen team members or family members become protected in their roles, which has the effect of keeping emerging leaders at a distance rather than embracing their new and better ideas. Another vulnerability is the megalomania or irrational self-centeredness of the original humble leaders who may convince themselves of their own brilliance rather than maintaining the openness and flexibility that led to their success in the first place. How much of this has already happened or will happen as Singapore ages remains to be seen.

Lessons to Be Taken from This Singapore Story

- The main leaders created a cooperative group who had open and trusting relationships with each other. This group could collectively plan and be accountable for the major structural changes they mandated and enforced.

- To create a new kind of open and trustworthy government, they created a long-range plan of developing the best talent in the country by creating careers that were comparable to what those alumni could have achieved in elite private sector positions.

- Open and trusting relationships were valued at every level of the governance structure and its associated economic and political structures.

- The short-term use of arbitrary power in governance can be justified if there is a serious socio-technical survival problem to be solved.

- A culture built around Humble Leadership is inevitably subject to drift as the organization grows, ages, and scales. Leaders need to be wary of the eroding forces of protecting people and conventions rather than protecting the Level 2 openness that catalyzes continuous adaptation.

> **Humble Leadership** empowered Singapore's heads of state to transform the country's economic development.

FOUR

Transforming a Medical Center into a Level 2 Culture

At this point in our analysis it seems appropriate to consider an entire organization moving toward Level 2 relationships in all interactions among staff, up and down the hierarchy, across occupational boundaries, and, most important of all, with patients and their families. Can an entire health care organization evolve and sustain what would amount to a Level 2 culture?

We know that health care is moving in this direction around tasks that require a high degree of coordination (Gittell, 2016). We know that many hospitals have adopted various versions of reexamining their work processes through different kinds of reengineering models, and we know that there are broad calls for the "coproduction" of health by involving patients and families in a more active way with health care professionals to improve overall "population health" (Nelson et al., 2007). We see clear examples of new collaborative models in the operating room (Edmondson, 2012) and in the emergency room (Valentine & Edmondson, 2015; Valentine, 2017). What we have in the case of Seattle's Virginia Mason Medical Center (VM) is a serious 15-year effort by the board, the CEO, and leadership to evolve the entire hospital culture toward Level 2 around the overarching value of *doing what is best for the patient.*

The VM story began in 2000 and has been thoroughly documented because of its importance in showing what is possible (Kenney, 2011; Plsek, 2014). Our analysis of this case is based both on these extensive write-ups of how this transformation was achieved and on many personal conversations that Ed has had with the CEO, Gary Kaplan, and various other VM executives over the last 10 years. Ed has also met with the VM senior executive group of 32 people on the topic of evolving organizational culture and managing change. These meetings provided firsthand data on how the top executives relate to each other.

Creating a "New Compact"

The transformation of VM began during a time of challenging financial performance. After a tenure of 20 years, the CEO retired and a new CEO, Gary Kaplan, was appointed. He was an internal medicine MD in the hospital and had shown great interest in improving VM's overall quality as a hospital. Ed first heard about the VM story from Kaplan in 2006 at a meeting of a seven-person group of senior hospital executives who had been invited into an annual 3-day "think-tank" discussion led by Jack Silversin and his wife, Mary Jane Kornacki, at their home in Rockport, Massachusetts. Jack was known in hospital administrative circles because of his workshops with administrators and key doctors to redesign what the "compact" should be between the doctors and the organization's administrators (Silversin & Kornacki, 2000, 2012; Kornacki, 2015).

Many change programs never get off the ground or fail because the underlying cultural values of the medical and administrative staff are in conflict with each other on many levels and they don't jointly own a vision for the organization's future. Silversin had helped a number of hospital systems by running intensive workshops focused on getting these groups coordinated by first developing a vision of the future that they did share and then having them commit to explicit and reciprocal expectations regarding what doctors and administrators would do to help the organization progress toward that future vision. Once such a new compact was agreed on, it required all parties to live by it, get coaching or help to do so, or—at some point when being out of step with new norms was clear—leave.

It was obvious to Gary that a major transformational change at VM would require the commitment and enthusiasm of his senior executive staff, both administrators and doctors. His intuitive insight into the need for something more than transactional Level 1 relationships was reflected in his decision to invite Silversin to interview key players, including doctors, to see if a new compact would be helpful to VM at this point in its evolution. After the assessment, starting the compact work required that the several hundred key doctors and administrators had to get to know each other more personally in a retreat setting to explore common ground, to consider what would be best for patient health and experience, and subsequently to begin to develop Level 2 commitments to each other. But that was just the first step.

Choosing a Change Methodology

Progress in VM's implementation of Lean, the Toyota production system methods, throughout the organization was often discussed at our annual Rockport meeting because of its demonstrated success, first, in building a new physician compact around making patient safety and the total patient experience the primary focus of the transformation and, second, in analyzing and improving VM work processes. Kaplan explained that soon after he became CEO, he was convinced that a whole system could not be transformed unless a single change model was adopted and taught to everyone who became involved in the change program. Having a common model with a common vocabulary and standard processes for managing change also enabled more rapid *personization*. Gary had learned about the Toyota production system from Carolyn Corvi, a Boeing senior executive who had been involved in the implementation of it at Boeing, and she had encouraged Gary to consider trying the same methods at VM. She subsequently became the Virginia Mason board chair. Serendipitously, on an airplane flight a VM executive had met a consultant who was an expert on these methods who offered to help Gary and his team to explore this further.

Involving the Board and the Senior Executives

Gary also concluded that getting shared commitment to a single methodology for the transformation would require senior people to really understand it and buy into it. Once he was convinced it was worth exploring the Lean/Toyota method, he took a number of his key physician leaders, administrators, and board members to Japan for a 14-day trip to observe how the Toyota production system had worked in the auto and several other industries in Japan. On the last day of that trip the group as a whole made the decision to go forward and introduce the methodology to VM.

Gary understood that they could not learn the system without seeing it operate and, thereby, beginning to imagine how this might help them in running a medical center. They would learn by imitation and identification initially and then by trial and error when they launched their own projects.

In a conversation in March 2017 Ed asked Gary how important it was to involve the board, and he reaffirmed that without board commitment he could not have sustained the new program over several decades, despite the ups and downs that resulted from market changes in the Seattle environment. His response was immediate:

> It is absolutely essential, which is one reason why I always took several board members along on the trips to Japan, which have become an annual event.

He continued with an important insight into the learning process and what it really means to have board support:

> It is not enough for the board members to *understand* the program and to *bless it*, because they will not really understand what is involved personally in some of these transformational changes that the doctors and administrators will have to go through *unless they have themselves had a personal learning experience which gave them not just insight but active enthusiasm for what was going on.*
>
> It was also essential that they understood and became familiar with the Toyota production process because without most of the organization learning the nuts and bolts of it, many of the changes could not have been achieved. *By going on these trips and learning together, they formed relationships that made the board useful as an essential support system.*
>
> It is now a requirement that all board members participate in this 2-week Japan learning experience during their first 3-year term in order to be eligible for reappointment.

Gary thus confirmed what we had learned over and over again in the many change projects we had observed and participated in, that such projects are often canceled in midstream, *even if they are succeeding*, because the board does not understand the transformation process and subsequently brings in a new CEO. If the new CEO does not understand the progress that has been made, all too often he or she will end up canceling or reversing the improvement process and regress to Level 1 relationships.

Implementing the System and Seeing Some Results

Gary also understood that a transformation could not be *imposed*, so after the trip to Japan, workshop experiences on improvement activities were key for physicians and all staff. Individuals began to see the relevance to their own work. Subsequently teams began to volunteer for improvement events and were asked to make proposals, get approval, and then learn the details of the Toyota system to get everyone coordinated. This activity and these events involved building Level 2 relationships with all the members of the organization that would be impacted by the proposed change, to ensure that they would understand and implement what was decided.

In US industry, the Toyota system usually had production experts observe the work, interview the employees about the work process, go off and redesign it, and then try to impose their solution on the members of the system, which all too often led to resistance or outright rejection of the experts' solution. To avoid such resistance in the VM projects, the leaders involved every level of employee, including doctors, nurses, techs, members of related functions such as pharmacy, and even patients and their families. This extended group of stakeholders helped to fine-tune and then to implement the new and better way of doing things *that they had helped to design.*

Gary emphasized that this worked because of the acceptance by all the senior leaders, and especially the board, of a shared goal that served as the ultimate criterion for whether a given proposed change was desirable or not: "Will this improve the quality of the total patient experience?" As obvious as this goal might seem in retrospect, when some of the working teams examined the system that had been in place, they learned that it had originally been built much more around the principle of providing the best experience *for the doctors.*

It was also recognized that many of the failures of change programs in industry had resulted from the administrative needs to cut costs and improve productivity through the various "reengineering" programs that had been developed, without considering the impact on the people, both as sources of information on how to improve things and as the workers who would have to use the new system designed by the engineers. The VM projects took the longer-range view that quality and productivity both increased over the long run when everyone was involved in the transformation program (Kenney, 2011; Plsek, 2014).

The VM cancer center redesign, for example, presented quite a challenge if the goal was to make it effective and comfortable for the patient rather than just focusing on the doctors and staff. That involved bringing all of the diagnostic equipment and therapeutic processes into a single area instead of having patients run all over the hospital to get diagnosed and treated. It turned out that to accomplish this goal, the space occupied by the dermatology center was ideal for the cancer center, which meant that the leadership team had to work with the dermatology department to get them to give up their space. This was accomplished by working with them on the design of a better space for themselves and often took intense relationship building over a period of months and years. This process highlighted the conclusion that such changes only work and last when all the participants have developed Level 2 relationships, have learned to be open with each other and trust each other's mutual commitment, and, most important, have been involved in creating and implementing the change.

This intensive approach over the next years enabled VM to transform many of its operations. For example, the emergency room was able to implement a process of sharply reducing waiting time and discomfort by providing immediate diagnosis and treatment. Primary care facilities were redesigned in ways to enhance a smooth workflow by co-locating several critical functions. Wards were organized around the nursing-patient interaction rather than nursing stations, to enable nurses to form better relationships with patients.

A patient safety alert system was created that was the medical equivalent of the Toyota production line process of "stopping the line." In the hospital situation if any member of the treatment group saw a problem, he or she could stop the treatment process to get an immediate review. These patient safety alerts promptly brought all relevant team members and their leaders together in one place to rapidly begin to understand the issue and what needed to be done. This stimulated closer relationships across the entire medical center continuum.

If diagnostic or treatment errors occurred, the process was to openly identify them so that the systemic causes could be identified and fixed, instead of the more traditional process of identifying a person to blame. By involving everyone in a climate in which it was often "safe to speak up," it was possible to identify the complex interactions that caused errors.

Based on direct observation and talking to individuals, it was clear that the overall program had achieved a climate of mutual trust across the top three levels of the organization, which enabled them to deal more constructively with the problem of interdepartmental conflicts. The high level of openness and trust in this group was the key to maintaining patient safety and high-quality patient experiences even as increasing economic and political complexity put pressure on the bottom line.

REFLECTION: FACILITATION AS HUMBLE LEADERSHIP

We tend to associate leadership with great new visions, and the VM story certainly illustrates that. Without Gary Kaplan's clear vision and dedication to making this transformation happen, the VM program like so many others would have stalled. It is important to highlight, therefore, that Kaplan as a humble leader also personally facilitated the implementation of his vision with a myriad of interventions that would be thought of as belonging more in the realm of process consulting, or "humble consulting" (Schein, 2016).

Our purpose in telling this story is to highlight what we consider to be a critical part of Humble Leadership—the mindset, the interpersonal and group insights, and the group skills that led to Level 2 relationships throughout the organization, all combining to make the implementation of the vision a lasting reality. Process decisions such as taking board members along on the trips to Japan are examples of building longer-range relationships that are essential for the new ideas and values to become embedded. We tend to mislabel those kinds of decisions as "facilitation" rather than seeing them as genuine integral acts of Humble Leadership.

In his earlier writing on process consultation and helping, Ed always noted that such facilitation and helping skills should be part of any leader's repertoire. What we are saying now in the context of complexity and interdependence is that such facilitation and helping skills have become a *major* part of what leadership is already, and such skills should increasingly be exercised at all levels of the organization. Career promotion in a hierarchy will have to be based as much on these interpersonal and group process skills as on technical know-how and volume of accomplishments.

We need to begin to take seriously this idea: Interventions, such as facilitation, coaching, troubleshooting, and catalyzing, are basic acts of leadership when they cause a workgroup to do something new and better. Humble Leadership involves convening and effectively managing meetings because effective meetings will be integral to problem solving (group sensemaking). We have to recognize that turning groups into teams, fostering collaboration, consensus testing, and conflict resolution have to be Humble Leadership skills. Much of what organization development consultants are asked to do in today's organizations will have to become basic Humble Leadership skills at all organizational levels.

The question always arises of whether such a profound transformation of VM could have occurred without a financial crisis to get the board's attention. Organizations that are relatively successful become increasingly myopic and fail to see potential problems until there is a significant cost overrun, a missed revenue quarter, a major accident and a death or two. Organizations are also very observant of what their competitors are doing and should be able to learn from that. Unfortunately they may then hire a visionary leader who is embedded in Level 1 leadership models who tries to make major changes with Level 1 top-down processes, shakes up the system, achieves some visible changes, leaves for a bigger job, and fails to notice that the culture has not really changed. All too often, the opportunity for change is squandered.

The Main Lessons of the Transformation

- The major lesson of the VM case is that the CEO began by building Level 2 relationships with his board and senior executives around a single goal: everything will be designed for patient safety and well-being.

- The CEO *personized* those relationships first by taking his executive team and some board members to Japan to experience for themselves the Toyota methods and, most important, learn together. Subsequent annual trips to Japan have included emerging leaders, doctors, and frontline staff.

- To ensure longevity of changes and support the new relationships, the CEO asked everyone to learn the same change methodology. Joint learning deepened the Level 2 relationships.

A health care CEO developed **Level 2 relationships with his board** and throughout the hospital to create transformational change.

FIVE

Humble Leadership in the US Military

Some form of hierarchy, a layering of formal ranks or implicit status levels, is intrinsic to all human systems. Hierarchy is a structural characteristic of organizational life, but what actually goes on between someone higher and someone lower is not automatically prescribed. We have hierarchies of administrators and professors in universities, senior partners and junior partners in professional service firms, committee chairs and levels of seniority in legislative bodies, differing levels of authority in large research projects, and, of course, clear levels of authority and rank in the health care system in which the operating room personnel function as a team with as many as four such layers.

The type of organization in which Level 2 relationships seem most out of place is the US military, where the very essence of the relationship is that you "obey your commanding officer's orders." This stereotype is largely based on military histories that highlight how important it is for Armed Forces personnel to learn to obey orders no matter how arbitrary or senseless. At the same time, those same histories contain many stories of individual heroes who chose to disobey orders because they made no sense in the actual situation and thereby saved their compatriots and/or won a key battle.

A growing number of stories drawn from recent conflicts emphasize teamwork, cooperation across hierarchical boundaries, and empowering the troops to make their own on-the-ground decisions (McChrystal, 2015; Fussell, 2017). What, then, is "command and control" in the military today, and how does it relate to Humble Leadership?

In other words, what actually goes on between someone higher and someone lower can vary immensely and is to a considerable degree a matter of how the higher-ranking person chooses to relate to those below him or her. Depending on the actual situation, a hierarchical relationship can be anything from Level Minus 1 to Level 3, but it has to be *at least Level 2* to facilitate trusting, open, psychologically safe relationships when complex tasks are involved and lives are at stake.

EXAMPLE 5.1. **Turning Followers into Leaders on a Nuclear Submarine**

We begin by summarizing some of the main points of the remarkable published account of transforming the culture of a nuclear submarine from a demoralized, marginally effective, "by the book" Level 1 hierarchy to a high-morale, effective, proud Level 2 organization with the basic philosophy of converting a leader-follower system into a leader-leader system (Marquet, 2012). There was still the military hierarchy, but there were not any followers; everyone was a leader in his or her own area of expertise. In telling the story, Captain

Marquet provides enough detail for us to see how much of this hinged on his evolving Level 2 relationships with all the people below him.

Marquet notes that the traditional Navy way is to take orders, follow tradition, and avoid errors. He approached the issue with a different mindset—to take initiative and seek excellence. In a traditional hierarchy the sailors learn to play it safe, avoid errors, and hunker down. Marquet saw that doing this had had the effect of keeping sailors out of trouble but had also resulted in low morale, low self-esteem, and only marginal performance. To build morale, the sailors would have to develop pride in doing an excellent job. Getting a group to this level falls to the initially appointed leader, who in this story saw that the submarine could be more effective and safe if the leader created a new mentality and new attitudes in the crew.

Marquet began building his relationship with his new crew by a lot of hanging around, talking to people, and asking a lot of questions because he actually was not familiar with this ship and his curiosity was, as a consequence, honest curiosity, rather than a rhetorical tactic. His "reading of the room" led him to the conclusion that the first change had to be made in his relationship to the people most influential in the ship, namely the chief petty officers (CPOs or "chiefs").

One way of building Level 2 relationships with his "chiefs" was to bring them together in a meeting and *personize* by humbly inquiring, "Are you happy with things as they are on this ship, or would you like to see a better way of doing things?" He reports that it took a lot of conversation and time to get the CPOs to realize that he meant it and was not just waiting to reveal his own hidden agenda. He notes, "Like so many times, my not knowing the answer ahead of time helped me. Instead of a scripted meeting where I pretended to solicit ideas, we had an honest conversation" (Marquet, 2012, p. 170).

The group had to get past justifying the old system of just letting senior officers "command and control." In the old system they felt safe but did not, in the end, feel accomplished. This led to the low morale and complacency around the work itself. However, the fact that they had not been rated well gave everyone an incentive to do better and, therefore, made them receptive to what Marquet was inviting them to think about. When things are seemingly going well, it is much harder to get an organization to take seriously that improvement can be made. The CPOs, through Marquet's inquiry, agreed that they were not really satisfied with how things were.

The next key question that Marquet posed was whether *they* saw any current procedures that *they* wanted to change. It is worth noting how much more empowering this question is than the suggestion of some changes that the officers or outside inspectors have identified. It is based on genuine curiosity, and presumably Marquet might not have guessed that the first such thing the chiefs wanted to change was the policy that all leaves of absence had to be approved by all seven levels of the ship's hierarchy, which often caused delays and, thereby, made family and personal time-off planning very difficult.

To change this process, and have only the immediate superior approve leave requests, was against what the Navy's "book" required, but Marquet agreed to try it, knowing that he was taking a personal risk by going against the book but also realizing that he was setting an important personal example of overriding regulations and tradition if they did not make sense in the current situation. The new system worked and was an immediate morale booster.

The CPOs learned that when they had ideas for change, they were expected to propose them, to overcome their complacency of waiting for orders, or their conflict avoidance, but instead to move quickly ahead in discussing changes with the captain and implement them if it made collective sense. To reinforce the attitude of taking initiative, Marquet changed the system of giving orders based on someone's suggestion by insisting that the direct report announce the suggestion in the form of "Sir, I intend to... (change course, increase speed, etc.)," to which the senior officer would respond, "Very well" if it made sense. Marquet further mandated that hierarchical language such as "request permission to," "I would like to," "what should I do about," "do you think we should," and "could we" should be replaced by "I intend to," "I plan to," "I will," and "we will" to train people to feel more empowered and specific in their intent.

Marquet also points out how the formal organization developed very precise jargon to improve the speed and accuracy of orders and thereby actually punished so-called informal conversation. He had to rebuild what he called "thinking out loud" and "stating assumptions" about proposed decisions, as necessary supplements to building trusting connections—ironically *to formalize informal communication.* Marquet trained people to precede their "I intend to" with stating why they thought that was the right move if it was a complex or controversial decision. Assumptions were only dangerous when they were silent and hence could not be tested.

Many organization theorists have argued that effective organizations achieve their goals because *informal* communication acts as a supplement and often counteracts misunderstandings or communication gaps that routinely occur in the Level 1 bureaucratic exchanges. Learning to speak openly has also become an important mechanism in "after action reviews" in which inspectors, senior officers, and crew members are equally responsible for saying what they observed and thought. On Marquet's submarine, all of these behavioral changes were taught so that critical information was eventually "embraced openly," which shifted the emphasis to improving performance based on more complete information rather than avoiding errors or assigning blame if errors did occur.

As the crew in the various departments of the submarine became more confident in exercising their own knowledge in the areas in which they were expert, they found it easier to pass that same power down to their own direct reports, so control and influence moved more and more to those who knew how to diagnose and fix local situations that would come up. Most important, as they felt more responsible, they saw more areas that needed improvement, saw ways of doing things better, and, in that sense, became leaders themselves. This illustrates well how a humble leader scales Humble Leadership.

Our argument that this reflects Level 2 caring for whole people rather than people in roles was suggested by one of Marquet's descriptions of wanting to explain to all the sailors some of the excellence goals that justified a new behavioral rule, which was to convey pride by greeting everyone who boarded ship with his or her own name, the name of the person boarding, and "Welcome to the ship." He believed that acting with pride would eventually lead to feeling pride. And the pride is in the person (who I am) not in the role (what I do), symbolized by stating one's own name and the name of the visitor.

To explain this, Marquet called the 100 persons of the crew to a single meeting in which everyone lined up according to rank, with the sailors in the back. He noticed that they were less attentive, realized that they probably could not hear him very well, and ordered them to come to the front and gather around him, a definite break with official procedure. This showed to even the lowest-ranking sailors that the commanding officer wanted each of them to hear the message, that each of them mattered, much as how in our surgical example (Example 1.5), the surgeon's slowing down the checklist or taking his team to lunch reflected that same intention.

In a traditional hierarchy, it is in the interests of the junior person to be Level 1 formal because it is safe to just do what the boss ordered and not to have to overthink or be too accountable. But if the higher-level person creates an informal, more personal Level 2 connection, and does so authentically rather than as a tactical exchange, this may create a powerful stimulus for the junior person to feel seen and taken seriously.

LESSONS

The most important lesson of this story is that it is possible to change a top-down control system in a hierarchy into an empowerment system without having to abandon the hierarchy. What is required is a readiness on the part of the organization to improve its operation and a humble leader whose mindset, attitudes, and behavioral skills consistently train the employees to shift from error avoidance to purposeful seeking of excellence. We also learn from this story that building readiness requires patience, persistence, and total consistency over a long period of time. In addition, Marquet's willingness to change some of the routine traditional procedures led to the discovery that the higher-ranking officers welcomed this new way of doing things rather than punishing Marquet for it.

A second important lesson is that this kind of change requires insight into and skill in managing group relationships. In his account, Marquet provides numerous examples of how the specific way he behaved is what made the ultimate difference in getting others to change their behavior and eventually their attitudes.

EXAMPLE 5.2. The Thunderbirds and "Drafting": How High Performance Depends on Very High Levels of Mutual Trust

Retired Colonel JV Venable provides in his book *Breaking the Trust Barrier* (2016) a detailed account of how the Air Force Thunderbirds are trained to be able to fly in close formations where planes are only a few feet from each other and, by flying very closely behind each other, can take advantage of "drafting." Drafting is the technique that birds and road racers use when one gets very close behind another to enable them to both conserve energy and move faster as a team than they could individually:

> Drafting, in teamwork, is a phenomenon that replicates the aerodynamic benefits of bodies moving closely together. It requires leaders to inspire closure between individuals and entities to deliver cohesion, unity of effort, and team acceleration.... The difference between high-performing organizations and those that fall short of the gold standard is not just talent but how well leaders develop their team's draft with the talent they have.... To harness the effects of drafting and bring trust to bear

within your team, you need to focus on closing the gaps. . . .
A gap is physical or emotional distance caused by a lack
of competence, a lack of confidence, or an unmet social
need that degrades performance. Left unaddressed, gaps
are momentum killers that will thwart any hope of trust.
(Venable, 2016, pp. 14, 17)

We could not have argued any better for the need to be at
least at Level 2 and maybe even at Level 3 in the work context
when complex, risky tasks are undertaken that require tight
coordination from all the members of the workgroup.

Col. Venable describes in great detail the various ways in
which he *personized* his relationship with the team members to build commitment, to ensure loyalty, and to build
mutual trust. For example, the 21-day onboarding process
emphasized new members' having to rely on each other in
various exercises to build "connective tissue." Various engagement rituals forced more intense listening to each other
and encouraged more personal revelations to each other to
speed up *personization.*

"Developing loyalty requires a foundation of mutual commitment, but the magic of loyalty relies on your getting to
really know your people and what makes them tick" (Venable,
2016, p. 69). Trust in this context then becomes "the willingness to put yourself or your team at risk in the belief that
another will follow through on a task, in a role, or with a
mission" (Venable, 2016, p. 119).

LESSONS

What this story points out is that "getting closer to each other"
is not just a socio-emotional issue but has its technical counterpart in the world of flight and racing. The Thunderbirds,
Blue Angels, and other high-performance aviation teams

depend on drafting to perform what they are trying to do, whereas in the business world it is more of a choice.

Returning briefly to Singapore, when we talked to Philip Yeo about his years of finding companies to go to Singapore, we got the impression that he defined his leadership success in very similar terms. Philip's boss pulled him in very close, and Philip clearly pulls his various direct reports and colleagues in very close, enabling them to be more effective. In the start-up world we see the same phenomenon with entrepreneurs and technical founders who drag partners and colleagues into such close "drafting" relationships and thereby are able to move faster and more effectively.

Another point that could be highlighted from this story is that the clearer and riskier the mission or task, the more important it is to form close personal relationships. Even the most professional experts functioning in a Level 1 role cannot be totally trusted, because it is much harder to anticipate what the Level 1 leader will do when the situation changes and the team is presented with unexpected threats or challenges. Professional distance creates opacity that interferes in volatile situations. This is why *learning* together in a simulated environment becomes a crucial relationship-building activity (Edmondson, 2012).

EXAMPLE 5.3. Building Level 2 Joint Accountability through a Clear Shared Goal: The Polaris Missile Example

Dave is the retired president of Lockheed missile defense systems. In his 40-year career from first-level engineer to technical and program manager and his last 5 years as president of the 8000-member missile systems division, he was involved in all of Lockheed's missile programs, including the original US Navy Polaris and each of its successors, Poseidon and Trident, as well as in the US Air Force space programs such as the Discoverer, the initial US satellite reconnaissance capability, and also in ballistic missile defense demonstrations.

Over several mealtime meetings with Ed, Dave recounted his experiences and talked about his own managerial style. The first head of the new Polaris program was Rear Admiral William "Red" Raborn, who established it and expected everyone on the program, whether contractors or government, to be members of a *military-industry partnership* and dedicated to the program's success with uncompromising integrity. He communicated his expectations for total honesty, admitting mistakes, and reporting bad news right away so that problems could be addressed immediately and fixed. This also meant making decisions based not on expediency or near-term profit, but rather on long-range life cycle cradle-to-grave results. The overarching goal was to successfully accomplish something that had never been attempted and do it within the constraints of commitments made to national leaders. Mutual commitment and integrity were the key underlying values, and *group accountability was taken for granted.*

Early in his career as a first-level flight controls design engineer Dave was involved in a complex multimillion-dollar system test to conduct a full-duration captive firing of the first fully instrumented Polaris missile. He had been working for several months with another test engineer to provide a program to inject commands during the test to cause the rocket nozzle controls used to steer and stabilize the missile to move back and forth throughout the entire 60-second firing. The goal was to measure the rocket exhaust deflections throughout the test, along with the response of the missile guidance system. The test was conducted, but the nozzle controls moved only 10 percent of what was planned. A large part of the test's purpose was not realized, and Dave acknowledged that he and his partner had miscommunicated on some key measurements that resulted in the failure. When a major review panel asked Dave and his counterpart to give an accounting of what happened, Dave said, "It was due to my mistake" because he felt that he should have caught the error. Owning up to his error was respected and built overall confidence in his bosses that he would tell it like it was. That personal experience demonstrated to Dave that the management emphasis on integrity was not just words but real, and he never forgot it.

Thirty years later Dave was president of the same missile systems division during the final development of the sixth generation of the fleet ballistic missile program, the Trident II. In reviewing those successful years, Dave emphasized both integrity and group accountability over and over again. When Ed asked him what he meant by that, it came back to being free to speak up, accepting errors and always facing the truth without reservation, and working together to establish program objectives. He then added with intensity that trust has to be continuously *earned*; it can never be taken for granted. "One should always be able to communicate without fear."

Dave's prescription: You can begin building trust within the circle of your influence by practicing and expecting integrity in every aspect of that area of influence. You set the standard and then discourage behavior that doesn't meet that standard. If people still don't live up to that standard after being counseled, you weed them out, remembering that no matter what managers write or say, they demonstrate their true intent by what behavior they reward and tolerate. You get what you settle for.

At the same time, you do your best to shield those who work with you or for you from the aberrations caused by the lack of integrity outside your influence. Even if you fail to succeed in maintaining that buffer, if you have earnestly tried, those who depend on your integrity will appreciate and respond to it. Others outside your influence will begin to see that result and be affected by it in their dealings with your group. Is this easy? No way! It is hard work to earn and maintain trust in the workplace. There are many conflicting pressures, and the job never ends. But the dividends are tremendous if you are willing to work at it and have the "courage of your convictions."

Dave said he was very fortunate to have belonged to an organization that valued openness and teamwork. As his responsibilities grew, he observed how different styles of leadership presided over meetings as problems were encountered and addressed. He found that openness and group participation encouraged teamwork and problem solving when they occurred. Where participants felt free to frankly disclose problems or issues without risk, corrective action plans often benefitted from knowledge and resources in other parts of the organization. While some of his direct reports initially preferred "short meetings with corrective action details left to subsequent one-on-one interactions," Dave believed that the "all in the same boat" analogy should be the guiding principle. When a leak suddenly occurred in one part of the boat, it might be one individual's responsibility to try and plug it, but the rest of the occupants of the boat would have an abiding self-interest in bailing to help avoid sinking. His staff and status meetings were therefore structured to encourage early identification and ownership of real and potential problems and development of coordinated action plans without shooting any of the messengers. When a problem was aired, Dave would ask who had the lead, if they had what they needed to determine solutions, and how other parts of the project might be affected.

Dave kept emphasizing that *joint accountability* was taken for granted and functioned well but was dependent on the high level of trust and open communication that they had achieved. Killing of the messenger was simply not tolerated.

LESSONS

We noted in Chapters 1 and 2 that managerial culture implicitly discourages groups and meetings, tends to disparage them, keeps them as short as possible, and perpetually complains about them as a necessary evil. In all our cases, especially Dave's missile program, we see leaders creating meetings as part of the problem-solving and decision-making process. They believe in meetings, learn how to hold them effectively, and train their peers and direct reports to value them. In doing so, Dave also illustrated his willingness to go against what his own superiors might value.

We also pointed out that managerial culture abhors "group accountability," yet we see examples of how, when goals are clear and when technological complexity requires a high degree of mutual trust and coordination of effort, such as in this missile program, a group can be held accountable and feels it, even when the system around it is looking for root causes and bad apples to blame when things go wrong.

The most important lesson from the point of view of Humble Leadership is, once again, that such leadership, well exemplified by Dave, is neither soft nor easy but possible when the complexity of the task requires it.

EXAMPLE 5.4. A Case of an Admiral's
Humble Leadership

We were recently told a memorable story by a retired US Navy admiral that illustrated how "collapsing" the hierarchy and opening the door to Level 2 relationships can sometimes be done quickly and decisively. The admiral, at the time, was in command of a nuclear-powered US Navy aircraft carrier. Effectively, he was the CEO of a 5000-person co-located organization for whom safety and high-quality performance would be top priorities. As a nuclear scientist and naval aviator, his background, experience, and hands-on knowledge suited him exceptionally well for the technical aspects of his mission, yet his instincts as a leader are what this story is about.

There was an incident on the flight deck in which an error in chocks and chains handling, a critical part of aircraft operations, could have endangered lives or caused the loss of very valuable naval aircraft. The error resulted from mishandling by one of the flight deck handlers (a "blue jersey" in aircraft carrier parlance) who reported up to an aircraft-handling officer (a "yellow jersey").

Given normal Naval hierarchy and protocol, this error would have been recorded, post-mortem debriefed, and corrected, and there would have been some degree of reprimand and disciplinary consequences for the blue jersey. The admiral told us that this was not outside of the normal course of aircraft carrier flight deck operations. Complicated things happen, and the US Navy has a few hundred years of organizational knowledge to deal with such incidents. That is, the commanding officer could have let the hierarchy work the problem and the solution, but that is not what happened.

Instead, he invited the blue jersey to the bridge to discuss the incident, just the two of them. One can hardly imagine how that junior chocks and chains handler must have felt, getting called up to the bridge, presumably to get reprimanded directly by the commanding officer. Knowing how critical these intricate details of deck and aircraft handling are to the safety and to the mission of an aircraft carrier, the commanding officer, a pilot himself, wanted to hear directly from the deck what had happened, perhaps why, and certainly how and why it would not happen again. At a deeper level, he cared more about the truth and the process, and far less about the discipline to be applied. The system would take care of that.

What must that meeting have been like? Was the blue jersey terrified, mortified, contrite, and reconciled? If all of those feelings were present, how would the commanding officer get to the truth of what happened? The admiral told us how he managed to quickly create what we would describe as psychological safety for the deckhand by focusing the conversation on his own curiosity of what had happened and why, making it clear that this meeting was not about punishment but about exploration. The shared goal was for that junior seaman to walk away from the meeting with a dedication to doing it better, not a reprimand for doing it wrong.

A reprimand would certainly reinforce a commitment to the hierarchy. As commanding officer the admiral wanted commitment to the task, to safety, and to quality performance. With the gesture of calling this meeting, and focusing the dialogue on the person and the truth, he reinforced his commitment to improving the processes that save (or could cost) lives on an aircraft carrier. The visible, personal two-way dialogue demonstrated a commitment to a process that the most senior leaders and the most junior sailors could identify with and learn from.

Stepping back from this case, small acts of Humble Leadership by the admiral may well have been a matter of course in his organization, a culture set by a senior leader that existed before and after this incident. This does not change the story except to amplify the truth that this admiral had a clear sense for the importance of *personization*, establishing openness and trust, even in a 5000-person hierarchical organization.

LESSON

What is most striking to us about this story is that the existence of a steep and formal hierarchy does not require the persons at the top of that hierarchy to behave in a transactional Level 1 manner. They can choose to *personize* at any time and at any level, thereby very visibly reinforcing some of the central values that they wish to highlight.

Summary and Conclusions

It was tempting to write this whole book around the amazing stories that are surfacing about Humble Leadership and the creation of Level 2 relationships in very hierarchical organizations. Retired general McChrystal in his *Team of Teams* (2015) and Chris Fussel in *One Mission* (2017) make it very clear that organizations now have to replace the efficiency of the linear industrial factory model with agility and adaptability as the problems they face become what we have repeatedly called complex, systemic, interconnected, and multicultural, that is, messy. Dealing with customers in an interconnected multicultural world will become as complex as dealing with fluid, invisible, polymorphic enemies. O'Reilly and Tushman (2016) make a similar point in their argument for organizational ambidexterity in that the economic and market forces are similarly fluid and unpredictable, requiring organizations to develop distinct subgroups that can respond differently as market and competitive conditions change.

McChrystal points out correctly that what makes the difference is not technological superiority but "the culture," by which he means the degree to which the troops are trained not only to be precise about those things that really need to be standardized, but to be able to think for themselves and self-organize in those areas that require a new bespoke response. The stories reviewed here are all built on that assumption, but we have added that "the culture" has to be a Level 2 culture and that transformation is only achieved by a certain kind of relationship building.

To create the agility needed to respond to a volatile and chaotic environment, McChrystal emphasizes empowering local units to be coordinated by a team of representatives from those units. The solution of having each team have a representative at a coordinating meeting to create "the team of teams" only works, however, if each representative has spent time in each team and established Level 2 relationships within each team. Otherwise it is inevitable that each representative would feel the need to argue for the values and methods of the team from which he or she came (in other words, digging in on one side of a technical, transactional negotiation).

In the last three chapters, the stories we have told are more "*socio*-technical" in their emphasis on integrating the human social issues with the technical workflow issues. In the following chapter, we will explore how too much emphasis on maintaining and instrumenting the technical systems can leave the social systems vulnerable and ultimately fallible.

> **Humble Leadership** creates and is reinforced by **Level 2 teaming** even in highly structured hierarchies.

SIX

When Hierarchy and Unintended Consequences Stifle Humble Leadership

The last three chapters illustrated what can be accomplished when formally appointed or elected senior executives choose to abandon Level 1 bureaucracy. But Humble Leadership is an activity that can happen even in the most rigid bureaucracies when an individual manager or employee sees an opportunity to do something new and better, and decides to act on it. We see Humble Leadership in many organizations when an individual manager chooses to treat his or her colleagues, direct reports, and even the boss in a more personal Level 2 manner. We see many managers who have discovered the power of Level 2 relationships running effective meetings, building strong teams, and launching efforts to proliferate Level 2 in other parts of their organization. Sometimes, however, it does not go that way, even with good values and good intentions.

There are three kinds of obstacles that we have observed: (1) managerial cultures resisting newcomers' efforts, (2) leaders unwittingly undermining their own efforts, and (3) new CEOs overturning improvement programs that are foundations for Level 2 cultures. What follows are examples to illustrate each of these challenges.

EXAMPLE 6.1. How Hierarchy Can Undermine Level 2: Brian's Story

Humble Leadership is potentially all around us and always has been, yet often it does not proliferate but is instead stifled either by regression to Level 1 or by organizational forces that result in a Level 2 manager leaving voluntarily or even being fired when the new CEO chooses to stay with more traditional management methods. It is unfortunate when this process defeats the organization's own efforts to develop its people, as the following example illustrates.

Brian was a few years out of college with an engineering degree from a top-tier program. He joined a prestigious yearlong rotational management training program at a large multinational food company. He was an outstanding performer in training sessions and gained a top spot supervising a packaging line in a large manufacturing plant.

This large food company is an aggressive marketer and decentralized manufacturer with many different brands marketed throughout the world, manufactured and packaged close to key regional markets. Brian was located at a plant in the center of the US. The leadership team at this plant has a lot of autonomy and is under a lot of pressure from headquarters to maintain rigorous production volume and quality standards. As might be expected, Brian's boss leaned on him hard to get the job done efficiently.

Brian's direct reports were mostly high school educated, unionized, diverse ethnically, and predominantly male. Brian was able to form open and trusting relationships with them in his first few weeks on the job. His management training during the past year highlighted the importance of good relationships with plant workers, and his personality led to casual friendly relationships even though the team had far more experience with and knowledge of the operation that Brian was tasked to lead.

The challenge came from the machinery involved in the line. Brian's assessment was that the machinery was not well engineered and was complex enough that it was difficult to figure out how to fix it when it broke down. With this unreliable machinery as the "elephant in the room," it is not surprising that Brian experienced asymmetrical relationships with, on the one hand, his team of unionized line workers and, on the other hand, his boss. When we asked him whether his subordinates would tell him when something was not working well, he said, "Absolutely, we talk all the time and do our best to figure out how to fix things. I have really gotten to know these guys; I know all their issues with the union, and we work well together to keep output and quality as high as we can."

When we later asked Brian whether he told his boss when things were breaking down or off schedule, he gave a different kind of answer:

> Absolutely not. All he wants to hear about is that things are working and that we are meeting schedules; when things break down, he just gets upset and wants to know who to blame. The reason we get so many breakdowns is because the packaging machine is not very reliable, yet the boss seems to think because I have an engineering degree, I should automatically be able to fix it. A lot of what goes wrong neither my experienced crew nor I know enough to fix. They should really replace the machinery, but my boss doesn't want to hear that!

Brian had built open, trusting relationships with the line workers but found himself in a professionally distant, competitive, if not antagonistic, relationship with his immediate boss and those farther up the management chain. He could not get across to them the problems with the machinery and began to realize that maybe they did not care.

How might we explain such asymmetry across only two levels in the hierarchy? Did senior management operate by the "conventional wisdom" that in traditional lower-skilled, lower-specialization, manual production work professional distance is necessary to maintain the authority to keep the plant humming at high utilization? Clearly Brian and his direct reports considered this neither conventional nor wisdom. Brian's relationship forged naturally with his team was peer-to-peer as much as it was boss-to-subordinate. Brian and his team understood who the boss was, and they understood that the problem lay in their situation, not in their relationship.

The opposite might be said for Brian's relationship to his boss. Brian could see that the more role-based, distant relationship built around measurement and production targets characterized the entire hierarchy above him. This made him consider, given his personality and his enjoyment of his work with his team, whether he should think about a different career. Brian also saw that his boss was indifferent to the situation and had no sympathy or empathy for the team's struggle with faulty machinery. With some reluctance, Brian realized that another similar manufacturing company would likely follow the same hierarchical patterns and decided instead to pursue graduate studies in an adjacent field that promised the possibility of different kinds of work in different kinds of organizations. Brian put it very succinctly: "I did not see anywhere in this organization any role models; I did not want to be like any of the people I was reporting to."

After 9 months on this job Brian gave his notice and left to go back for a master's degree in engineering with the hope that he would end up in a more interesting, forward-looking organization. After investing a full year in training Brian, the company lost a high-potential manager by revealing a rigid, measurement-oriented, cost- and schedule-dominated system that the unionized workers had learned to tolerate but that immediately turned Brian away from what had seemed like a dream job. Brian was trying to be a humble leader. He was succeeding with his direct reports, but the traditional hierarchy above him was operating on a fundamental Level 1 transactional leadership model. This raises an interesting question: How representative is Brian of a new generation (we will risk labeling him a "millennial") who expect to be led in a different way because their worldview and mindset seek to lead and be led in a different way?

LESSONS

The most important lesson of this story is that different parts of an organization may have different goals resulting in different kinds of incentives for managers at different levels in the hierarchy. Headquarters may evolve an excellent plan to identify and develop future general managers but "forget" that the present middle management is not motivated to develop people. The most telling comment in Brian's story is his saying that he did not see any role models in the company.

The second lesson is that, even when Brian felt safe enough to tell his boss that the machine was technically the source of the many breakdowns, he was ignored. Consider the absurdity of this outcome, given that Brian had been hired for his engineering talent. Creating a climate that encourages people to speak up is of little value if the system does not have the capacity to hear and react appropriately to what is said. We associate that inability to hear and adapt with Level 1 transactional role relationships.

EXAMPLE 6.2. Good Intentions, Transparency, and Unintended Consequences: The BCS Story

This is a story about a Silicon Valley start-up that lived and died a few years ago. (It is based on a real situation but is an amalgam and is adapted, embellished, and "sanitized" for the purpose of illustration.) It's not an unusual story in that the company was well funded, well regarded, well run, spirited, and excited, with breakthrough technology and experienced people. It is also typical in that, in the end, it was not able to pivot, adapt, and innovate its way to sustainable independent growth and prosperity. Most of the employees were well compensated and had significant financial upsides (shares of common stock). And most of them learned a lot before losing their jobs and realizing none of that equity upside.

MANAGING WITH TRANSPARENCY

The communications systems company we're calling BCS provided enhanced communications technology to medium-sized enterprises. The company was founded by tech industry veterans (engineers) who knew how to create new solutions. In order to build a business based upon this novel approach, they hired an experienced chief executive who had been successful building other technology start-ups. The CEO brought in another experienced sales and marketing executive to complete the senior management team.

The founding product designers and their hired-in professional managers shared the value of managing with objective fairness and transparency. They had all seen too much subterfuge and "political behavior" in their past lives at large companies. They also shared the value of wanting to demonstrate honesty and integrity to their employees and to their board of directors. Integral to this transparency was a metrics-based management system. They decided that all of the functional leaders would define their key metrics, around which they would manage, be managed, and be evaluated thumbs up or thumbs down. The data would be presented to the company on wall-mounted LCD displays—a real-time pulse of the business on full public display.

Employees found this fair and had no reason to doubt or question the direction set by senior management. Transparency was a foundation upon which trust, up and down the management chain, could be built. The artifacts of a culture of transparency and candor were abundant at BCS. One could walk into the main room, crowded with tables and workstations for everyone from customer service to engineering to marketing and executive management, and see the LCD screens on the walls with real-time metrics of business performance. A few times per month, the company would offer lunch, typically from a favorite local pizza place, and use the "all-hands" opportunity for candid discussion of how things were going, what needed attention, who had been hired, what birthdays were coming up, all things for everyone to know.

In addition, senior managers would take rotations of employees, from all parts of the organization, out to more selective curated lunches to stay in touch, get to know each other, and share information. For anyone joining BCS at this time, candor and transparency would certainly have appeared as important espoused values. BCS employees appreciated the day-to-day presence and involvement of the senior managers. When they got together, they felt that it was okay to talk openly about their wins and losses, their success and failures. This included everyone from the newest hires to the CEO.

For the CEO and senior management, transparency was as important for upward communication as it was for downward communication. Senior management at BCS wanted to express the state of things to their board with as many real-time metrics as possible. Why not use network technology, social and streaming media, and so on to provide the major investors with a real-time console of all the information they wanted and certainly deserved to know? This seemed like a sensible and fair way to manage a small and growing enterprise. And it was, while things were going well.

Somewhere around the second or third year, BCS hit a plateau. Transparency notwithstanding, there were some disconnects between the product team and the sales teams struggling to close deals with target customers. For the CEO, managing by the numbers was what he had been brought in to do. And the numbers were now clearly indicating who was meeting the targets and who was not.

A CONSEQUENTIAL DECISION

In a decisive move, made after deliberating with other board members and founders, the CEO acted upon the performance data by terminating the employment of one of the original product founders, who was not getting the product line to where it needed to be. The CEO hoped that this core personnel move would improve the pace of new product delivery and demonstrate to the organization the importance of acting decisively when the metrics suggested action was necessary. It was tough for the CEO and everyone else, and a bit of a shock to the system, but it was what the numbers said. No hiding from the truth; it was what it was.

About a year later, BCS was sold at a loss to a larger company and downsized by over 50 percent. The CEO and his management team believed they had done all the right things about setting strong anchors—communicating strong underlying values around hitting their metrics and maintaining transparency. It had seemed like a very healthy modern company. What had gone wrong?

A year or two after the company was sold, a senior member of BCS noted, "After one of the founders was terminated, everything changed." The long-term impact, presumably an unintended consequence, was that a culture of Level 2 relationships and trust was betrayed by transactional by-the-number management. This calculated risk on the part of the CEO underestimated the damage of taking such abrupt authoritative action and, thereby, introducing an *insidious substrate of fear.*

The market had shifted for BCS, their solution was not perfectly aligned to market needs, and the company could not thrive given this shift in the external environment. It is hard to know whether this was *because* fear and the erosion of Level 2 relationships prevented the company from creatively pivoting. Nonetheless, it is clear that the introduction of fear, betraying a climate of trust, did not help.

LESSONS

Many managers, leaders, and theorists have highlighted the importance of transparency, especially this century, but most have also conceded that opening up all the channels for all kinds of work-related and financial information is far easier said than done. It is also the reason why we prefer the concept of "openness" to highlight that *what* and *how* we communicate is not a passive process of making things visible, but an active sharing, revealing, listening, understanding, and responding process. Transparency can be a passive process that does not discriminate what is perceived unless deliberate filters are built in. We know that we rarely want to see everything. Openness is a choice of what is important to reveal to get the job done, not just the metrics of what happened and when.

The CEO and other senior managers at BCS were trying to build trusting Level 2 relationships. But after one of the founders was fired, the value of sharing and acting on performance information really reflected a different foundational assumption favoring tough-minded, individualistic, mechanistic, pragmatic, transactional leadership (Level 1). Here transparency and candor were quite consistent with a tacit assumption about individuals in the organization being free to do their own personal best, to self-optimize, to compete on equal footing (using the same shared information), and to accept the "broad daylight" consequences of their actions and transactions.

Did such deep assumptions about individualistic, pragmatic, transactional relationships prevent them from continuing to build the Level 2 relationships that could have ameliorated the climate of fear? Was trust something "nice to have" but not an intrinsic management value? Transparency without trust may well keep employees engaged and motivated, and possibly very productive, for a period of time. Yet we've all seen the backstabbing, political, hide-the-ball, deceive-your-peers-to-stay-ahead atmosphere that some leaders may implicitly encourage as the requisite prescription for hypergrowth companies. In the long run, however, with such transparency as a means of control more than as a means of communication (openness), companies trend toward entropy as disillusioned talent leaves, the wrong kinds of skills and performance are promoted, and creative pivoting in response to market changes becomes politically controversial. Intrinsic openness and trust, Level 2 relationships at all levels of the organizations, make a far more flexible and enduring substrate than the endemic fear of transactional Level 1 metrics-driven management.

We believe teams of all sizes perform better when team members feel psychologically safe to be open with each other. Whether we label it a climate of fear or the loss of psychological safety at BCS, it likely dampened the spirits, undermined openness, and threatened the company's ability to innovate and pivot. Protecting psychological safety might have resulted in slowing time to market in the short term but might also have increased resiliency in the long term.

EXAMPLE 6.3. The Paradox of Level 2—Stable in the Individual but Not in the Organization: The Organic Car-Design Story

We have encountered numerous leaders who inform us that once they have Level 2 relationships with their direct reports and teammates, they find it so satisfying that they cannot imagine leading any other way. We have also encountered numerous leaders who tell us that they were able to create Level 2 relationships in their organization only to discover that a new CEO brought in above them preferred the more traditional Level 1 professionally distant, technically precise management methods, including transparency, formal metrics, and clear norms of managing strictly by job descriptions and well-articulated targets, reinforced by "carrots and sticks."

The preference for the Level 1 transactional approach often reflects comfort level with tradition and sometimes a genuine failure to understand what Level 2 is and can do. For example, one of the major projects undertaken by the Society for Organizational Learning was to discover whether the sequential linear process by which cars were designed could be made more efficient, cheaper, and shorter (Senge et al., 1994; Roth & Kleiner, 2000). In the traditional design process, if a change was made in the chassis, it might affect the space available for the engine, which might thereby permit a larger engine. If it weighed more, it would affect the design of the tires and so on, so redesign would be perpetual, sequential, and expensive and take forever.

In the late 1990s, Rob, a systems-oriented project manager charged with designing a new 1995 Ford Motor Company model, decided to do something different and better. He learned group and systems dynamics and realized that a linear process was inappropriate for such a highly interdependent design. Rob then built Level 2 relationships with the managers of each stage of car design and convinced them to attempt a team-based design program in which the 100-person design team could try to work as a co-located organic group rather than an assembly line. To even move in this direction meant overcoming a great deal of skepticism both in the higher-level managers and in the designers themselves, but they discovered that as they got to know each other and learned how to work in teams, this was indeed faster *and much more satisfying.*

The design was viewed as a complex multifaceted problem where things often looked out of control initially, but once people could openly discuss the implications of each of their design ideas and proposed changes, positive resolutions came very quickly. As in the case of the Polaris missile design group (Example 5.3), the shared learning and high mutual acceptance made the group collectively accountable. There were many large and long meetings to iron out the multiple contingencies in the system. At one point, a senior executive walked in on one of these large meetings where multiple design issues were being discussed at once, concluded that this "experimental" group was totally out of control, and sternly ordered Rob to "get the project under control or it would be discontinued." Rob "promised" that he would get the group under control but did not change any of the team's group approach, in part because by then the team itself could see how much more efficient and productive their work was. The result was a dramatic completed new design many months early and well under budget!

The car was a success, and the company, not the design team, took credit for it by explicitly announcing that the design team had been "out of control" but that senior management had successfully gotten them under control. Rob was convinced that senior management believed that and that they never realized an entirely different design process was the cause of the success. In the meantime, Ford was undergoing a "resizing" program, and Rob and many of the team members were on a list to be let go as part of this program, were given no credit for this success, and were eventually terminated. The design processes went back to the sequential linear method. Rob, along with a couple of his former buddies from the project team, went on to form a consulting company to teach systems thinking and team building by means of experiential workshops.

LESSONS

How important is it for the executives above an innovative project to fully understand, not just to condone, the innovation? We pointed out in the Virginia Mason Medical Center case in Chapter 4 that the CEO made a special effort to involve the board at the level of understanding and personal learning. One implication in the car design story is that Rob perhaps could have worked harder to develop a Level 2 relationship with his bosses, who clearly never understood the potential of a more relationally connected Level 2 design team. Rob's superiors were clearly made so uncomfortable by seeing a large group in dynamic interaction with each other that they reverted to a more comfortable, familiar command-and-control mental model.

It is clear that if senior management neither understands nor condones a new way of doing things, the project is vulnerable. What is disturbing in cases like this is that the organization does not understand how its own ignorance or misunderstanding stifles its future capacity to innovate. To be able to pivot to something new and potentially better requires management to have at least a mental model of what that might be, even if the appetite for implementing the change has not yet developed.

EXAMPLE 6.4. The Impact of New CEOs

A different scenario with similar outcomes can occur when a CEO launches an improvement program, supports it while he or she remains in the job, but then moves on to a different organization. The new CEO, with a different mandate, explicitly or implicitly withdraws support, kills the program to streamline the organization, and either fires or reassigns the key architect. We have seen this happen to a number of programs that were successfully launched using the methods of the Toyota production system (Lean). To be done correctly, it requires building Level 2 relationships with the employees of the microsystem that is redesigning itself to be more effective (as was done so successfully at the Virginia Mason Medical Center, discussed in Chapter 4).

Two programs we have worked with were progressing toward building Level 2 relationships between key doctors and administrators as part of a broad program of improving all the elements of patient care and experience. In both cases the CEO sanctioned and approved the improvement programs in the main hospital but was personally more involved in a broader strategic effort to increase the size and scope of the whole medical program in the region by acquiring local clinics and expanding services regionally. Both the acquisition program and the improvement program required building administrative and organization development staffs, the costs of which began to outrun projected income. In both cases, the CEO went on to another job, leaving his replacement with a financial shortfall that required immediate cost cutting and downsizing.

Not surprisingly, one of the first things that was drastically reduced was the improvement program. An important corollary program to create doctor-administrator pairs was canceled, and a large number of the organization development consultants who had been hired were let go, stopping much of the improvement work in midstream. In both cases, the senior leaders and some of the middle managers who had championed the programs, who were acting as humble leaders, found that they could not personally accept the "regression" to a Level 1 culture and left to join other organizations that were more ready to implement the improvement programs. For example, a director of nursing who had created a Level 2 climate in her whole nursing organization was fired but found another hospital in which she began to create a similar program. These "migrants" either brought with them other humble leaders or set about to create Level 2 cultures in their new jobs.

LESSONS

The most important lesson is that once one has made the transition from Level 1 to Level 2 relationships, the new environment feels more comfortable, more real, and more effective in getting work done. The humble leader therefore finds him- or herself in a difficult position if the executives above don't understand, don't condone, or don't support the relational and team activities that the humble leader advocates. *It is an unfortunate reflex during a financial crunch for the managerial culture to cut slower-moving and expensive investments in building relationships and teams.*

A number of hospitals are finding that the experiments to build Level 2 relationships between medical and administrative staffs are showing promising results. If they invest in Level 2 relationships, they subsequently find it much easier to resolve issues of redesign of the various medical and administration services because they learn to tell each other what is really on their minds. They work hard to find common ground instead of settling for lowest-common-denominator compromises. Yet these kinds of long-range investments in relationship building are often cut.

When we see successful projects of this sort, we also discover that the real driver of challenging traditional assumptions and Level 1 relationships is the growing complexity and multifaceted nature of delivering health care. Gittell's (2016) work on relational coordination has helped many organizations to begin the improvement process by focusing initially on identifying the *role interdependencies* because even the purely technical side of delivering health care has become highly interdependent. Her research has found that an important first step is to identify those role interdependencies and then to ensure that the people in those roles become aware of their common goals, learn of each other's work, and learn to respect each other even if that cuts across occupation cultures and status levels. Both the experiences of patients and the medical outcomes are improved if the doctors, nurses, pharmacy, administration, and lower-level technical staff begin to see themselves as an *interdependent* system.

An unresolved question in the various projects that have been launched on relational coordination is whether shared goals, mutual knowledge, and mutual respect supported by frequent appropriate communication is enough, or whether these various role actors have to evolve Level 2 relationships for the system to function optimally. This dilemma is well illustrated in some research done on ERs where one of the improvements was to organize the relevant doctor and nursing roles into "pods" that would work entire shifts in a more interconnected manner. That meant inevitably that the members of the pods would get to know each other better and form something akin to Level 2 relationships. In her research on four hospitals that were experimenting with pods, Valentine (2017) found that it worked well in two of them where the team members believed that the assignment to the pod and the scheduling would be administered fairly, but the two other hospitals rejected the experiment because potential team members feared that there would be cheating in assignments and scheduling. That suggests that if the broader hospital culture is stuck in Level 1 rules and roles, the suspicion of cheating and lying immediately comes into play. Level 2 relationships, encouraging such *personizing* in a subunit, may not work if the higher levels do not understand or condone the concept.

GROWTH AND BALKANIZATION

In addition to what was noted in "The Evolution of Roles and Relationships: Growth and Hubris" in Chapter 3, there is another force that can undermine Humble Leadership as companies grow—balkanization. We like this descriptor because it captures the dynamic nature of groups as they grow in size and number. Not only are we referring to competition or polarization between groups, which obviously can happen when increasingly complex organization designs follow growth in product lines, sales, and profitability, we are also referring to the intense loyalty and "we/they" thinking that develops *within* groups. It is not simply competing for scarce resources between groups; it is the strong belief that "what we have in our group" is special and should be protected. The internally focused Humble Leadership in one group can erode that openness and trust upon which the larger integrated organization was built in the first place.

There are many cases of this in the past histories of technology companies, with DEC, discussed in Chapter 1, and Sun Microsystems being two examples. DEC experienced such balkanization between first-generation PDP computer design teams and subsequent-generation emerging teams who worked on a different technical platform. Simply put, Ken Olsen was not able to bridge the divides once the scale of the company exceeded his ability to scale Humble Leadership across all of the subgroups. His Humble Leadership in the early days of a single mission-driven innovator was not possible to sustain between engineering groups that were competing with each other.

The situation at Sun Microsystems was similar in the mid-1990s when groups representing ardent beliefs about, for instance, large symmetric multiprocessing systems, open-source software, or engineering workstations, to name just a few, were contending for resources and mindshare to such a degree that the company went through a design iteration with "planets," distinct divisions that would manage their own profit and loss before "rolling up" to the integrated Sun whole. As with DEC, one can look at the Sun case through this lens: the Humble Leadership that provided the initial impetus for the company (energy and commitment built on strong, trusting Level 2 *personization* among the founders) was eroded by an inwardly focused group mindset that seemed more committed to ardent beliefs within the division than to the original mindset that propelled the larger mission of Sun as a whole.

Ultimately it is the humble leaders' challenge to reinforce both the autonomy that small teams need to innovate and the Level 2 connections within *and between* the divisional leaders who are necessarily brought on as organizations scale up. It may be very natural for a newly hired leader to relate to new peers in different divisions with Level 1 transactional "professional distance," effectively reinforcing balkanization. We think it is critical in such growth phases that the CEO and board themselves develop and model Level 2 relationships across hierarchical and divisional lines, as was the case in our industrial (Chapter 1) and military (Chapter 5) examples and in the case of the Virginia Mason Medical Center (Chapter 4).

Perhaps the toughest challenge for Humble Leadership is to avoid both group hubris (we/they) and Level 1 transactional distancing that can deepen intergroup conflict to the point that *what started as growth ends in entropy.*

Summary and Conclusions

In this chapter we have tried to illuminate how Humble Leadership and working at Level 2 occur throughout various parts of the organization. We see founders experimenting with some aspects such as transparency, we see middle managers redesigning their units, and we see experiential programs springing up to help administrators and professionals to learn together as a precursor to developing Level 2 relationships. But traditional managerial culture based on the *lone hero* and the *machine model* is deeply embedded, so we also see many examples of failed efforts followed by regressions to transactional Level 1 approaches.

Ironically, the single best indicator that Level 2 and Humble Leadership can proliferate is that messy complex problems are becoming more common, and the importance of growth is as high as ever. Both forces combined may compel the present leadership to move toward Humble Leadership in order to strengthen their organizations' ability to "see" and adapt in order to grow.

We close this discussion with an interesting recent observation made by the chief of medicine of a major hospital during a lunch discussion of "doctor burnout." He noted that in his experience with the various doctors in his hospital, those who had more personal relationships with their patients were *less* burned out than those who had more formal transactional relationships.

> **Humble Leadership** can work anywhere in an organization but is vulnerable to senior executive lack of support.

SEVEN

Humble Leadership and the Future

As we are exploring the future of relationships among individuals and groups at work, we have to think even more broadly about the future of work itself, to consider how our concepts of Level 2 relationships and Humble Leadership will prove to be necessary for sustained effectiveness. In this chapter we will focus on six ways in which Humble Leadership will coevolve with trends we see impacting our work lives in the next few decades:

- **Context over content**: Humble Leadership will be even more about *context* and *process* and less about *content* and *expertise*, in part due to the growing impact of artificial intelligence.

- **Cultural heterogeneity**: Humble Leadership will have to cope with tribalism and build relationships unbound by unconscious biases.

- **Distributed power**: Humble Leadership will have to challenge individual abuse of power.

- **Mass customization:** Humble Leadership will help groups become more agile, adaptive, and collaborative to tailor leadership to employees, stakeholders, and customers.

- **Dynamic organizational design**: Humble Leadership will have to perpetually reconsider how to organize relationships and workgroups in a global mobile world.

- **Virtual presence**: Humble Leadership will involve being both physically present and virtually present as organizations become more globally distributed.

Humble Leadership Will Be Even More about Context and Process and Less about Content and Expertise

It should come as no surprise that a discussion touching on the future of work would start with some agonizing about the impact of artificial intelligence (AI). We join many who expect that large swathes of economies, entire segments of industries, and significant categories of work will be permanently altered or eliminated by distributed clusters of microprocessors "thinking," making decisions, and directing work. There is little doubt that some categories of work will be more vulnerable than others. Broadly, we believe transactional work (for instance, trading in capital markets) can gain so much from AI that the "trader" role as historically defined might have to be considered vulnerable.

If we are correct that transactional roles may be more vulnerable to AI or augmentation, the challenge will be to redefine the vulnerable roles so that human, contextual processing, that is, building resilient Level 2 relationships, will be what is rewarded rather than content and transaction management.

There is another way we see Humble Leadership skills as important in an AI-augmented future. What people think they know will be worth less than it used to be. The *leader as a visionary expert* reaches a point of diminishing returns when *anyone* can access the same information and when doing something new has more to do with the implementation processes at play in the organization than with information deficits or expertise gaps. If everyone knows or can know, leaders are no longer sole experts, they're just one of the crowd, or one in the cloud!

This diminished power of the sole expert results, in part, from the ubiquity of AI and the skills of those trained to exploit it. Neural networks built on unlimited processing power (virtually infinite cloud computing power and storage) will continue to appear more and more "intelligent." Most of us have experienced how search engines have nearly perfected their ability to finely predict, accumulate, customize, and animate the concepts we search. This trend will likely continue to accelerate as more natural interfaces to AI (e.g., "Alexa," "Ok Google," or "Siri" queries) augment information and make it even easier to assimilate the nearly unbounded collected human knowledge, especially when there is commercial value associated with such augmented-reality micro-targeted assimilations. In other words, humble leaders should accept that access to and distribution of information may no longer have much power in maintaining a command-and-control hierarchy.

Even today, the pace at which databases are tapped and mined for immediate and nearly complete answers to questions is staggering, especially when the database access is in the hands of "digital natives," who started learning to search at age 10 or younger. An employee a decade or two from now, trained in data science, adept at latest-generation query languages, and, of course, facile with an ever more powerful mobile networked device, will have a substantial information assimilation advantage over older digital learners. This gap may be widened further by Kahneman's (2011) observation that older "experts" tend to become overconfident in what they "know" (have learned) and dismissive of their own ignorance, what they have yet to learn. The young curious AI-augmented digital learner may quickly develop a wider and fuzzier knowledge set that is more adaptable, if not more relevant, than the deeper but bounded knowledge of the older experience-bound "expert."

In *Thank You for Being Late*, Thomas Friedman suggests that our common experience of artificial intelligence will be as IA, or intelligent assistance (Friedman, 2016, p. 199). This is an important framing, as it reminds us that generally automation does not mean the end of jobs; it means different jobs and possibly improved jobs. Humble Leadership can build on intelligent assistance by enhancing the ability of humans to process how information applies to particular *contexts* and in relationship to complex tasks. Within a few years we may find ourselves in distributed teams that share very advanced skills in accessing and processing AI-enriched information but without knowledge of how to align all of that data to the objectives and capabilities of a given team or across teams that need to collaborate. It is well known that the more information we acquire, the more gaps we see that require even more clarifying information, often leading to "analysis paralysis." Humble Leadership will be needed to orchestrate the group sensemaking process, to create the context for fully open dialogue, and to select the appropriate decision-making process.

Can we go so far as to say that AI augmentation and big data will become so powerful as to yield "AE," or artificial expertise, and should we worry about that? We do not think so—while AI or AE may be very efficient at ferreting out the *known* unknowns, it will be with Level 2 relationships, collectively muddling through uncertainty by *sharing, reading, and reflecting each other's reactions*, that Humble Leadership can provide the resilience to deal with *unknown* unknowns.

Humble Leadership Will Have to Cope with Tribalism and Build Relationships Unbound by Unconscious Biases

We are writing at a time when polarization in politics, socio-demographics, and economics is almost unbelievably high. And we are writing from a place (Silicon Valley) where gender discrimination and sexual harassment in innovative companies, large and small, are shockingly prevalent, considering how otherwise forward-leaning so many young companies are in this place and time. It is not our goal to suggest solutions to these deeply existential problems, except to offer this idea: Humble Leadership is built on Level 2 relationships that develop between whole persons who see beyond or around their unconscious biases. The development of effective Level 2 relationships, by definition, is nearly impossible in the context of discrimination, exclusion, and harassment.

The Humble Leadership challenge will be to leverage the intrinsically more tolerant attitudes evident in 20-to-30-somethings today into more effective globally distributed teams in the coming years. It is likely that 20-somethings a decade or two from now will find connecting digitally natural and easy, regardless of native locations around the globe. Productivity obstacles from different time zones, languages, ethnicity, race, and gender are likely to be lower 10 years out than 10 years ago, but the challenge to convene cooperative and productive groups will remain.

If we are correct in seeing the decline of explicit segregation and unwarranted exclusion, the unconscious biases that we all learn as we grow into our various "tribes" are still active, leading to various subtle and emerging ways of excluding others that we may not even be aware of today. Humble leaders will need to find a way through their own biases because true Level 2 relationships will not develop if a leader's unconscious biases interfere with her or his ability to establish trust and openness with employees, teams, boards, stakeholders, and so on. If unconscious biases nudge emergent leaders away from seeing the other whole persons and toward maintaining professional distance at a Level 1 transactional level, the influence of those leaders will likely erode, and they will be replaced by others who have learned to see through their biases and develop Level 2 relationships with an unbounded diversity of whole people.

Humble Leadership Will Have to Challenge Individual Abuse of Power

Leadership almost always implies using some form of power to make something new and better happen. Abuse of such power by narcissistic individuals is not a phenomenon limited to traditional strict hierarchies. Emergent humble leaders with better ideas must face their own temptation to think they are superior to others around them, especially in situations where they do outrank their prospective followers. This is compounded when pace is increasingly valued, creating the temptation for leaders to make hasty power moves. As Jeffrey Pfeffer notes in *Power* (2010), power abusers often succeed in the short run, and Adam Grant in *Give and Take* (2013, p. 5) also observes that, in the short term, "takers" (selfish power abusers) sometimes succeed because they believe they are playing in a zero-sum game, where one's gain necessarily means another's loss.

Humble Leadership proposes that self-centered abuse of power is never successful in the long run, despite individualized reward systems that favor selfishness over selflessness. The challenge in reaching Level 2, however, is that once megalomaniacs, iconoclasts, and "heroes" have abused power in the belief that they alone can solve a problem, it takes much longer for the acts of Level 2 successors to rebuild connectedness and trust. As Robert Sutton points out, bad behavior is five times more powerful than good behavior (Sutton, 2007, p. 170). By implication, positive leadership acts of mutual trust and openness must outnumber negative or bad acts by five to one to maintain optimal work relationships. It may be relatively easy for leaders to act badly toward a colleague that they out-rank. It may be easy to act badly toward a colleague with whom they maintain "professional distance," or toward whom they feel "indifferent." It is, however, much harder to act badly toward someone with whom they have established a *personized* Level 2 relationship.

We find it very encouraging that in early 2018, recent abuse of power scandals (sexual harassment in particular) have triggered a new awareness of a tipping point beyond which we can no longer accept abuse of power as "normal" (Carlson, 2017). Going forward, we hope to see far less risk of reprisal and retribution for standing up to abusers of power in what is referred to as "a growing culture of accountability" (Farrow, 2017). Our hope is that the benefits of Level 2 relationships and this growing intolerance for abuse of power will reinforce a Humble Leadership mindset that builds influence on trust and openness rather than on selfish short-term power plays.

The frequency of people standing up to say "enough is

enough" is increasing, reaching from industry to media and entertainment, and grudgingly to national politics (at least in some parts of the US political fabric). Digital natives (late teens and early 20-somethings) also remind us that social media provide such rapid information flow, such as light-speed public shaming that becomes de facto social justice, that bad behavior has nowhere to hide and the reaction to it is swift, powerful, and shared globally. We see Humble Leadership contributing to this zeitgeist emphasizing tolerance, respect, and the value of personal connections between whole persons.

Humble Leadership Can Help Groups Become More Agile and Collaborative to Tailor Leadership to Employees and Customers

The *bespoke* trend, everything made-to-order and delivered direct-to-consumer, is going strong in 2018, and we are confident that this leaning toward mass customization will continue for the foreseeable future. Unit-of-one customization at global scale is becoming commonplace in apparel, cosmetics, pharmaceuticals, IT, "medtech," "adtech," and so on. While 3-D printer manufacturing in the home is only for a small subset of the population, the idea of moving final manufacture and assembly for the individual consumer into the neighborhood, local mall, or generic shared office space is not all that far-fetched. We are already seeing variants of this today with unbundled low-cost airlines, food trucks, and pop-up stores, not to mention bespoke Tesla automobiles sold direct from shopping center show rooms.

Customization not only means tailoring of goods and services to individual needs, but also less waste in the long run. We think it is likely that *bespoke everything and waste nothing* will be very important in the minds of most employees in future-seeking organizations. Personalization is becoming mission critical for HR as they tailor benefits and incentives precisely to the personal needs and interests of each employee. Generally, we think it is likely that competition will drive many enterprises to respond directly to the unique demands for custom products and services, for which distribution will necessitate highly effective communications channels to share information flows and move local market decisions directly to where customers express unique preferences. Level 2 cultures that are built on unencumbered bi-directional information flows will be in a much better position to meet the demand for the wide variety of bespoke products and services delivered direct-to-consumer.

Building a network of personal relations that open the critical interfaces between people in an organization implies that static, defined roles in the organization may fall out of sync or may counteract productive Level 2 relationships. Relationships rather than roles may be the first pivot points to optimize in designing and redesigning organizations. *Humble leaders will need to* personize *in order to personalize.*

One way of characterizing self-managing teams is that they form backward from the desired customized output. These Level 2 overlays function by combining unique cross sections of skills and personalities and rely on open, trusting relationships rather than on chains of command. This kind of organizing sounds chaotic yet has already developed in some industries that are trying to turn VUCA (volatility, uncertainty, complexity, ambiguity) into advantage. Leadership skilled in the design of relationships backward from the goal of meeting a unique customer need may be much better prepared than leadership that is focused on maintaining order within the lanes. If the market is demanding customization, the leadership task will be to assemble "high-performing teams" (Ricci and Weise, 2011) of skilled players with the agility to deliver customization and continuous adaptation.

Humble Leadership Will Have to Perpetually Reconsider How to Organize Relationships and Workgroups in a Global Mobile World

Centralized organizations and authoritarian personalities constrained by certainty will not succeed in a world twisting toward distributed everything. (Johansen, 2017, p. 148)

In the immediate future, we see more organizations best described as "shape-shifting organizations" (Johansen, 2017) in which antiquated command-*and-conceal* transactional exchange behavior will not be rewarded, and leadership will occur organically not hierarchically. Hierarchies will still exist, yet they may come and go (Johansen, 2017), and the energy in organizations will emerge from the edge where cooperative relationship building is more important than who works for whom. In our view, Level 2 trust and openness become the critical connective tissues binding leaders and followers from an organization's edge to edge.

Ultimately, the future brings more moving targets and learning to cope with them. In Example 5.1 we referred to the book *Turning the Ship Around* (2012) in which Marquet made the special point that his goal was to turn leader-follower relationships into "leader-leader" relationships to symbolize how everyone had specific knowledge and context about something on the submarine and, in the end, they all had to be leaders in their own areas. If we think of them as humble leaders, they will have all been able to seek information and help from each other at any time, ensuring that everything functioned well, pursuant to their common goal. This suggests that one of the key questions of Humble Leadership, something that any crew could ask at any given time, is "Can we review what our objective is right now—what are we trying to do?"

In group dynamics and meeting management training, this is described as "testing goal consensus." It must become an important Level 2 process in any workgroup for someone to inquire "Let's check on whether we are all on the same page—what are we trying to do?" and to do this in a global geographically dispersed organization. Global mobile networks make this technically possible, yet the leadership challenge will be to facilitate group reflection and group sensemaking, which must build at least common understandings across linguistic and cultural boundaries.

Humble Leadership Will Involve Being Both Physically Present and Virtually Present as Organizations Become More Globally Distributed

One of the most consequential decisions a humble leader will need to make, now and in the future, is the degree to which physical presence is required to establish and maintain Level 2 relationships with direct reports and key contributors in an organization. We believe it will always be the case, even in the shape-shifting organization, that senior leaders will need to spend in-person hands-on time at the edges of their organizations. However, the mythical roaming C-level executive who today may need to travel 30 weeks a year away from the home office in order to *personize* and maintain connectedness with remote branches may in the future feel less obliged to be physically present all the time. For the rest of the organization, we suspect the cultural pressure to be "seen in the office, at your desk" will also likely decline in the decades ahead.

A few years ago, Marissa Mayer, CEO of Yahoo, made news by rolling back a work-from-home program that many employees loved but that was also deemed to be diminishing effectiveness in the organization (Swisher, 2013). It was an interesting milestone as Silicon Valley has cycled through waves of experimentation with flexwork, remote office, hoteling, audio/video conferencing, and so on. The Yahoo mandate from Mayer was one of the indicators at the time that the pendulum might be swinging back to favor effectiveness in the office over efficiency from home. Does this "pendulum" find a comfortable place in the middle? Now, only a few years later, we see even more reason to believe telepresence, augmented virtual presence, may provide that middle ground that leaders need.

We see this trend as, in part, a reflection of the possibility that the technologies to connect people and teams over networks will be augmented by sensors and big data in ways that could make telepresence as or more effective than actual physical presence. Another factor that may also aid the effectiveness of telepresence is the workforces who use it. We are pretty sure that younger employees at work 10 years from now will be adept at using mobile technology to communicate instantly and completely with their work and personal networks. We think it is worth considering that part of the headwind we have seen to full-scale adoptions of telepresence solutions may be the people, not the technology. Older employees at work today (we will risk labeling them "baby boomers" for now) represent a rapidly diminishing cohort replaced by digital natives who will likely find embracing telepresence technologies easy if not rewarding.

As an example of new telepresence technology that may

change our perspective, we should revisit how AI might add new benefits: specifically, will we see "reaction-sensing AI" as part of virtual conference room technology? Consider a networked conference room in which a team leader could conduct a meeting in real time, at any time, and from any location. Augmenting a real-time meeting with storage and replay might allow the team to have a better sense of the feelings and reactions of others in the room. Sensors plus AI that detect feelings already exist. Group/audience feedback systems are widely deployed. Could we improve the in-person experience by allowing anyone to review reactions of every team member at key points, or controversial points in the discussion? We will always have limits to our ability to read the room if we are limited to being in the room, but who knows what compensatory reaction-sensing technologies may provide—even better data about "the state of the room"—that being physically present might miss.

A sentiment dashboard based on sensors rather than voluntary input starts to feel like it could breach privacy or propriety thresholds. Johansen refers to an "uncanny valley" where technology such as automatic sensors that judge sentiment might go a little too far and not be adopted (Johansen, 2017, p. 106). Before getting to that sentiment-sensor "uncanny valley," meeting augmentation could still improve the flow of information, particularly on a tough subject in a contentious meeting. A humble leader will need to hear from all voices in the room. He or she may have established the right tone, the psychological safety to provide for unfettered bi-directional information exchange. Still, the tendency of some to be the loudest voice in the room, this common group phenomenon, is not going away anytime soon. Meeting augmentation with telepresence systems might easily ameliorate such an awkward meeting after the fact by providing feedback stored for later reflection and not skewed at the moment by that loudest voice in the room.

One thing we believe telepresence will not augment is the *initial* establishment of trust and openness. We will still need that human personal connection, the bond that forms in the off moments, in interstitial conversations, "at the water cooler," in the hallways, at a pub after work. It is the frequency of in-person time managing the deliverables of others that we suspect may decline in the next few decades. This amplifies our view that one of the key skills of the emergent humble leader is rapid *personization* to quickly establish open communication at those times when groups are co-located, in turn allowing an increasing frequency of times when telepresence is more efficient. Ideally, Humble Leadership builds on *personization* that leverages physical presence for co-creation of momentum more than for correction of miscommunication.

Summary and Conclusions

The best way to summarize these ideas is in terms of the basic dimensions that have informed our Humble Leadership model (see Figures 7.1 and 7.2).

Business history provides numerous examples of the heroic innovator who proposes something new and better. The image of the go-it-alone innovator, risking everything with extraordinary confidence and perseverance, will remain central to our heroic leader myth. What we question is whether this model of the alone-at-the-top chief decider, where "the buck stops," will remain as salient in the future.

In innovation-driven industries, where VUCA is accepted reality, we believe that as a company matures, the isolated, heroic leader will ultimately suffer from lack of complete information to make the right decisions. We have argued that what distinguishes the humble leader, at any level of the organization, is talent at developing optimal Level 2 relationships that seamlessly provide more and better information flow required to innovate at high pace.

An individualistic, competitive, destiny-is-in-your-hands-alone mindset limits a leader's ability to handle uncertainty and volatility, since no individual will be able to process the volume of data nor assimilate all the dynamic inputs that are vital to effective strategy. Brilliant, creative, charismatic iconoclasts will still step forward to propose something new and better. The future we see, however, is where this leadership brilliance is expressed more in "we together" cooperation than in an "I alone" delusion, particularly as organizations grow and become more diversified.

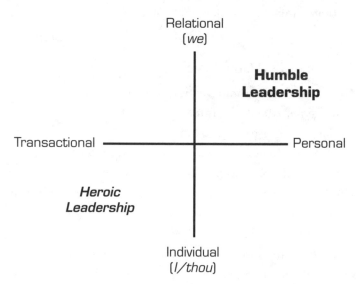

FIGURE 7.1. The Leader Perspective

Figure 7.2 takes the organizational perspective: We see roles (bottom of the vertical axis) that define the hierarchy (left of horizontal axis) and the respective lanes of activity as of secondary importance to the humble leader's Level 2 relationship *overlays*. All organizations face ebbs and flows of budget surplus and deficit. This invariably forces competition between divisions and functions for allocating tightly controlled resources. The roles themselves represent defined budget allocations ("Can we afford one more product manager?"). In this context, professionally distant relationships between roles across divisional lines are entirely appropriate ("Schmooze just close enough to be ready to co-opt their headcount in the next reorg").

In the upper right of Figure 7.2, the emphasis is on dynamic relationships between flexible groups. By "living sys-

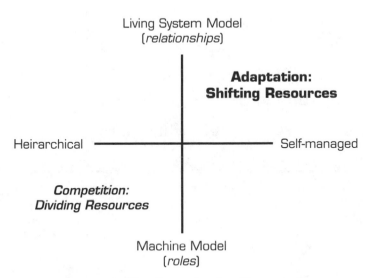

FIGURE 7.2. **The Organization Perspective**

tem model" we are describing an organization that responds to externalities by rapidly shifting resources (think of a body dynamically directing blood flow to the muscles that need it). The system responds holistically and cooperatively, shifting energy on the fly, regardless of roles, to adapt to a new threat or opportunity. By allowing the affected part of the organization (the body) to respond in the way that best fits the immediate need, the system lets the affected part manage its own resources and regulate its own energy use. Shifting resources dynamically is key to the system's success.

Humble leaders are there to "read the room," both the situation and the people involved, then to set the direction to something new and better given the volatile circumstances, and then to strengthen the Level 2 relationships that ensure complete information required to enable *the flexibility to never stop adapting.*

> **Future leadership** can fend off disruption with an adaptive, inclusive, organic organization design.

EIGHT

Humble Leadership Requires Reinforcing the "Soft Stuff"

We noted in Chapter 1 that something new is "in the air." What we see that is new is growing acceptance that managerial culture needs to be centered on interpersonal and group processes—colloquially, "the soft stuff." In the various stories in Chapters 3 through 6, we described how leaders had what we would label a Humble Leadership mindset and how their success resulted, in most cases, from their Level 2 skills in managing groups. The way in which leaders convened groups and then provided the incentives and experiences to make them into high-performance teams is striking. When the focus is on interpersonal relationships inside organizations, it is inevitable that group dynamics will become the critical variable in determining optimal task outcomes. The future demands that we evolve technical rationality into *socio*-technical rationality.

Learning to think in interpersonal and group process terms becomes a foundational building block of Humble Leadership. That implies even learning from the performance arts, where process is crucial to successful performance, as well as broadening our criteria of "success" or "winning" to include more qualitative criteria such as "total system performance" or "effective adaptive learning." The quantitative measurement focus suits the linear machine model, but as work becomes more organic and systemic, the way we evaluate outcomes must incorporate new perceptual if not emotional criteria suited to the complexity of the work.

The linkage between leadership and group dynamics is not new. Social psychologists studying organizations learned early on how powerful group relations are, and how much more work gets done when employees are working together rather than working alone. The power of group motivation has been well established in various experiments that highlighted that the best way to increase group energy and motivation was to have the group compete with another group. Much is known about the positive and negative effects of group forces under different task and contextual situations (Schein, 1999). However, we were so focused on how to improve motivation that we put blinders on when it came to seeing the various correlated consequences inside the group, such as becoming more autocratic, shutting down deviant opinions, going into unnecessary hurry-up decision modes, and generally undermining the diverse forces in the group that led to better ideas.

Focus on Group Process and Experiential Learning

Interest in group dynamics was stimulated by the theories and experiments of the German sociologist Kurt Lewin, who launched the Research Center for Group Dynamics and a doctoral program at MIT in 1945. What was really new in the research launched by Lewin was the profound discovery that the *subjects* of research could usefully become involved in the research process itself, what has since come to be known as "action research." Not only did group members provide vital data that the observing researchers could not see, but the involvement in the research process gave those group members profound personal learning experiences. A strong link was forged between generating knowledge and immediately applying that knowledge to the problems being investigated, especially in the field of education.

This insight led directly into experimenting with the learning process itself. Suppose the learners had the primary responsibility to learn and the teacher's role was to provide a learning environment and tools, but not the syllabus or readings? This method would obviously have limitations in the hard sciences, but might it be the key to learning the soft stuff, the dynamics of relationships, groups, and culture?

It was discovered that teaching and learning about groups and interpersonal dynamics could indeed be greatly enhanced if the teacher, instead of "telling," asked students to have real-time experiences and analyze them with the help of the teacher. This process of co-creation came to be what we now call "experiential learning" and led to the founding in 1947 of the National Training Laboratories where T-groups (T for *training*) were launched in Bethel, Maine, as the centerpiece of human relations labs on leadership and group dynamics (Schein & Bennis, 1965; Schein, 2014).

What is today known as organization development (OD) grew out of these early experiments with sensitivity training where managers and facilitators working together learned how *systematic analysis of group process* was needed in order to make sense of the events that occurred in and between groups within an organization. Today, one of the main organizational problems managers cite is how to get what are now called "silos," different divisions, product groups, or geographic units to work together. How would a "group process" emphasis help? In the human relations labs, we created groups and had them interact with each other in simulated communities or in competitive exercises and could observe how tribes formed within a matter of days and how quickly dysfunctional competition arose among them. Going forward, we could experiment with how to reduce intergroup tensions or how to co-create groups that would be more cooperative if not synergistic from the outset. Just as the learning process was co-created in the T-groups, so the design of organizations, groups, and teams could be co-created by the conveners and members of the group rather than an outsider expert. We learned from the outset in the T-groups that such co-creation always hinged on building relationships first, and that meant getting to know each other as individuals through *personization*.

We also learned that managing change, solving problems, and fixing organizational pathologies depended on making the participants aware of group process through reflection and analysis in simulated situations or designed "exercises" that made group issues and processes visible. A humble leader could create the conditions for such change by co-designing new group experiences as the following examples illustrate.

EXAMPLE 8.1. A Process for Getting Silos to Work Together

Saab Combitech, the technical division of Saab, consisted of six different research units, each working for a different

These examples were originally reported in *Humble Consulting* (2016) and are adapted for our purposes here.

division of the company. The CEO hired Ed as a consultant to design an activity that would make the heads of these research units recognize the potential of collaborating instead of functioning as independent units competing for scarce resources. Ed and the CEO designed a 3-day process-oriented workshop for the top executives of the six units around three segments (Schein, 2016).

In segment one, Ed would explain the concept of culture and how to decipher it. Each group would then designate two of its members to become "ethnographers" who would, in segment two, go into each other's groups to learn about each other's cultures and then, in segment three, would report out their findings to the total group. They could then collectively discuss where there were cultural themes that were common and could serve as the basis for developing more cooperation. The impact of observing each other with a cultural lens and being forced to talk to each other about what they observed created a completely different kind of conversation that led to many forms of cooperation over the next few years.

What made this work was the joint design with the CEO. He understood that he wanted the key members of each of the six units to get to know each other better, to begin to build Level 2 relationships, but instead of just having them do something together, it proved to be more powerful to make it a learning exercise: "Lets learn about each other's cultures" was a great objective when the implicit goal was to learn how to operate in synergy, across silos. The CEO also understood that he *owned the intervention* and made his needs the driving force.

For Ed as the consultant, the high degree of Level 2 *personization* with the Saab Combitech CEO empowered the CEO and Ed to challenge the different heads of the silos to work openly and leave out the mistrust that characterized the past rivalry between the silos. This experience with the Saab Combitech CEO also recalled for Ed his early interactions with the CEO of Ciba-Geigy (CG), the Swiss Chemical MNC now owned by Novartis. Early in building the relationship with Ed, the CG CEO invited Ed to spend a night and a day of conversation at the CEO's personal home in the country. While unsettling to Ed at first, it quickly became clear why this accelerated the work process in Ed's engagement with CG. The Level 2 connection, accelerated by spending time in a personal context, built trust and provided for openness that was critical in getting the change work done.

EXAMPLE 8.2. Creating a Different Organizational Process at the Massachusetts Audubon Society

The Massachusetts Audubon Society (Mass Audubon) was a large, successful wildlife and land conservation organization that had been operating for a long time throughout New England. Ed had been on the board for about 2 years when Norma, the head of Mass Audubon, and Louis, the chairman of the board, decided that it was time for a campaign to raise capital funds. Such a campaign had been run a decade or more previously, and the need for new buildings and expansion of the programs was growing rapidly. The big question was whether the board was ready to tackle such a campaign, because it would require a great deal of extra work and commitment from the board members and the organization's staff.

The process committee decided that they needed to create a task force of committed board members to address the question of whether or not the board was ready and asked Ed to chair this task force. He agreed and took it as a challenge to see whether using what we now call a Humble Leadership approach could influence how this task force of ten board members would work together on this campaign.

Ed's plan as task force convener was to let the group get acquainted informally over a meal with only the vague mandate that they would be discussing whether or not the board and the organization were ready for a capital campaign. That required overruling Norma's desire to open with a speech on how previous task forces had functioned. She also had to agree to starting with an informal dinner at a local club that would stimulate *personization*. During dinner, Ed kept the conversation general but then, over dessert, proposed the following with emphasis and gravity:

> To get our discussion going, I would like to ask us all to do something that some of you might find a little different, but I consider it very important to start in this way. I would like each of us, in the order in which we are sitting, starting to my left, to take a minute or two to tell the group, from the heart, why you belong to Mass Audubon. I would like no discussion or interruptions until we have heard from all of us. We can then proceed with our formal agenda. This will take us a while, but it is important that we hear this from everyone. Roger, why don't you begin? Why do you belong to this organization?

The logic behind doing this kind of "check-in" was to get everyone to say something personal. The purpose of asking people to talk "from the heart" was to *personize* their membership and, at the same time, to gather information from which to infer how committed the members of this task force might actually be to a capital campaign. If enthusiasm in the task force was missing, they would have to consider postponing the whole idea.

This process brought a new level of cooperation to this group. Each person spoke with great passion about how important Mass Audubon was in his or her life, how important its role was in conservation and nature education, and how enthusiastic each one felt about helping the organization grow and prosper. By the end of a half hour, everyone had spoken, and it was clear that this task force was ready to proceed with the hard work of involving the rest of the board and especially the employees and staff of Mass Audubon.

The task force of senior leaders then decided to replicate this "check-in" process with the respective staffs. Each of the leaders of the staff groups was asked to say why he or she worked for Mass Audubon, and the board members repeated their statements. We learned later that one of the most significant unanticipated outcomes of these meetings was that for the first time the larger staff actually heard ten board members say why they belonged to Mass Audubon. Until that time the staff saw these board members as only names with unknown levels of interest in the organization. Furthermore, as we had anticipated, the staff for the first time learned a great deal about one another's levels of commitment and interests. The organization had been plugging along with a Level 1 formal-role-determined process and had never really had a session where more personal feelings, motives, and values could be leveraged.

What started out as a relatively minor intervention turned out to have major impact because it *personized* the whole process of working together on the capital campaign. The campaign itself took off with personal connections, emotional engagement, and great enthusiasm and over its 2-year period successfully met its multimillion-dollar target.

The great contribution of this kind of *experiential learning* was to give people in organizations personal insight into how group processes worked and how important the understanding and management of such processes were to accomplishing the tasks that the groups had undertaken. In subsequent debriefs, groups could then collect further insights and develop the process skills needed to actively manage the group's work.

Group Growth and Development

Group performance depends very much on how the groups are created and the norms that are evolved around psychological safety for all members. A leader trained in group dynamics should understand how groups develop around the specific tasks they face. How well the group works reflects the kinds of relationships that are fostered in the initial group meetings, and this dimension of leadership is too often ignored in the mainstream of "leadership development," which emphasizes the special skills required for individual leadership excellence rather than skills required to make group members feel psychologically safe and to build a group culture that is adapted to the group's purpose. The humble leader needs to be aware of members' needs to develop their identity in the group, to learn how they can contribute, and, most important, to develop understanding and acceptance of the others in the group. This process typically fails when leaders push groups into task work too quickly, that is, before enough *personization* among members has occurred, hence trust and openness remain at a marginal Level 1, and collaboration looks more like exchange than cooperation.

Making Group Dynamics a Central Leadership Responsibility

We are proposing with Humble Leadership that we empha-size the concepts and vocabulary around group building, group maintenance, group development, and internal and external group relations that highlight how group members play many different adaptive roles at different stages of group development and that group boundaries will shift unpredict-ably as organizational work will shape shift. Leadership and followership become subsidiary role descriptions relative to the recognition of the important group roles and functions that make groups more or less effective: *convening, setting goals, evolving norms, asking for ideas, brainstorming, build-ing systemic understanding, identifying possibilities, decision processing, summarizing, consensus testing, action planning, and group sensemaking.* Our point is that these should not be topics and skill development areas for group specialists and consultants, but should become defining skills of the effec-tive humble leader.

We should also remember that early group research showed the very real distinction between *task* leaders and *relational* leaders in group evolution (Bales & Cohen, 1979; Hackman, 2002). We should not ignore the stages of group development that determine whether the group's problem solving will be valid or, as in "groupthink," will reflect the private agendas of certain members. Humble leaders need to be aware of how easy it is for a group to slip into collectively doing what in fact no one wanted to do because no one felt the complete psychological safety to speak up and no one had *the skill to test for consensus.* Here we are referring of course to the well-documented and all too familiar dysfunction known as "the Abilene paradox" (Harvey, 1988).

It is important to see this issue as a matter of *skill*. Humble Leadership involves skills and experience to know when and how to intervene with summarizing, consensus testing, polling, and, finally, decision making and action planning.

Humble leaders also must be wary of the tactic of applying efficiency criteria to the running of meetings, including publishing agendas ahead of time and, even when *new members* are at the meeting, starting the discussion immediately, keeping to tight schedules, in essence running a meeting much like a machine would be operated. Why is this a mistake? Because inevitably when individuals enter a new group, such as when they attend a meeting with new people, each participant will be pulled in conflicting directions: One force is the self-conscious thoughts about why we are there, what will be expected of us, how psychologically safe will we be if we speak up, and what hidden agendas or "elephants in the room" may be impacting effectiveness. The other force will be the relentless pull of meeting efficiency, to manage the time precisely, to reinforce the implicit hierarchy, and to drive progress through judicious if not brutal assignment of action items and deliverables. What is left in between these forces is the adaptiveness and organic energy of a group learning how to sequence a continuous stream of new tasks if not new priorities.

Especially if this is a new group or a meeting with new members, a better approach always is to begin informally with a gathering (not a meeting, but perhaps a free lunch, or doughnuts and drinks for everybody) and an informal check-in that allows people to calibrate themselves and get to know each other a little bit. Food and drink automatically put everyone on the same plane as humans "breaking bread," which becomes essential if psychological safety is to be nurtured.

We should not ignore that even a mature group has to maintain and nurture itself to be able to connect with and function in a network of groups, build connections with other groups, and develop the agility to deal with unexpected events that may require different kinds of leadership, followership, and membership behavior (Bennis & Shepard, 1956; Bion, 1959; Schein, 1999).

Summary and Conclusions

When all is said and done, we have to accept that leadership, culture, and interpersonal and group dynamics are intertwined conceptually and behaviorally. This is the *socio* of the socio-technical system; this is the "soft stuff" that humble leaders cannot delegate to HR, outside consultants, or facilitators. This is the stuff that is all too often ignored or actively pushed under the rug in Level 1 transactional management cultures. *It is once again (or perhaps always has been) time to bring the soft stuff into the mainstream of management and leadership.*

We all have the capacity to live and work at Level 2 and even Level 3, but we have not incorporated it sufficiently into work situations that require it. *Personizing* is challenging. Living in a transactional role-bound world of work is easier. We have to give it up because we will not be able to get the job done without *personizing* and building effective cooperation and team learning.

Emerging humble leaders will realize that their effectiveness will depend on their own understanding of this Level 2 soft stuff and their skill in managing it. They will learn this from their own experience, from consultants, and from their own engagement in workshops and various training activities. However, in the end, they must not only understand it, but own it. We believe that, in the end, leadership in complex organizations will be Level 2 *personized* Humble Leadership.

We can provide a little help in how to get there by describing, in the next chapter, a bit more precisely the necessary mindset, attitudes, and behavioral skills that are involved in becoming competent in Humble Leadership. We can suggest some readings and exercises, but we want to be clear that our own learning in this area has been experiential and that understanding of group and interpersonal dynamics requires experiencing those dynamics, not just reading or hearing about them.

> The **essence of Humble Leadership**
> is maintaining acute focus on
> interpersonal and group dynamics.

NINE

Personizing:
Building Level 2 Relationships

As we have said from the outset, most socialized human adults know how to build Level 2 relationships in their families and with friends. You have *personized* but may not have thought of it as a special mindset, attitude, and skill. You also may not have had the occasion to purposefully develop Level 2 relationships at work.

Our purpose in writing this book is to move readers to think as much, or more, about the *process* of building relationships at work as they do about the *content* of the work itself.

We think of Humble Leadership as requiring a certain kind of mindset, certain attitudes toward working with others, and skills in working with groups. We think of the learning process in each of these domains as consisting of three parts:

1. Some focused *reading and reflecting*

2. *Homework* at your desk designing work relationships

3. *Enhancement of behavioral skills* through fieldwork and experiential learning—by yourself or with others

Part 1. Reading and Reflecting

In this section we will present a number of references to other bodies of related work that will deepen your understanding of Humble Leadership.

EXERCISE 9.1. READING

Below are some of the major examples of parallel research and conceptual models that reflect emphasis on group process and the dynamics of complex systems. We suggest reflecting on and pursuing further learning about particular points of interest in this Humble Leadership ecosystem:

- Douglas McGregor in his classic *The Human Side of Enterprise* (1960) articulated "Theory Y" as an optimistic view of human nature that people want to work and accomplish things. The job of management is to create the conditions and provide the resources for work to get done. Too much of managerial culture is built on the cynical "Theory X" that people do not want to work and have to be motivated, given incentives, and controlled.

- Karl Weick in his *Sensemaking in Organizations* (1995) showed how sensemaking is a basic process that individuals and groups have to learn because raw experi ence does not provide the meanings and signals that may matter most. Group sensemaking has become a crucial process in high-hazard work such as in nuclear plants and in fighting wildfires but is, of course, equally relevant in any work that is complex and collaborative. See also Weick & Sutcliffe, *Managing the Unexpected*, 2007.

- Erving Goffman is his books *The Presentation of Self in Everyday Life* (1959), *Behavior in Public Places* (1963), and *Interaction Ritual* (1967) lays out brilliantly the subtleties of human relationships and group dynamics and, in the process, teaches us to be conscious of what we always do so automatically. His analysis makes society's cultural rules about Levels 1, 2, and 3 abundantly clear.

- Peter Senge in *The Fifth Discipline* (1990) showed how *systems thinking* is crucial to the "learning organization" and through the Society for Organizational Learning has been training managers in organizational learning and systems thinking for decades through experiential workshops that delve deeply into relational thinking.

- Otto Scharmer with his *Theory U* (2009) and the concept of "presencing" has redefined different levels of mindfulness and shown how conversation reflects the many degrees of connection with our own and others' deeper thoughts, as well as how deep connections and joint reflection are the only bases for the transformative change that leads to new behavior.

- Bill Isaacs in *Dialogue and the Art of Thinking Together* (1999) has brought us a whole new way for groups to interact with his evolution of Bohm's (1989) concept of dialogue by talking around a campfire and emphasizing suspension of our reactions instead of giving in to the "loudest voice in the room" or knee-jerk responses in a conversation.

- Amy Edmondson in *Teaming* (2012) has provided us with extensive research and cases of how important it is in building teamwork to *learn together* because in the learning process some of the dysfunctions of hierarchy are ameliorated.

- Jody Gittell in *Transforming Relationships for High Performance* (2016) argues for a "relational coordination" model that quantifies the strength of the linkages between roles and people, putting the relationship, not the individual, at the center of performance measurement.

- Frank Barrett in *Yes to the Mess* (2012) provokes us to think about how improvisation in a jazz orchestra comes about quite naturally because leadership rotates organically and unpredictably. In a similar vein, Powell & Gifford in *Perform to Win* (2016) show how an executive group can redesign itself through considering the leader-group interactions as *ensemble* performances in theater, in an orchestra, in a choir, and in pair dancing.

- Frederic Laloux in *Reinventing Organizations* (2014) describes the historical evolution of organizations as leading to the more organic forms that we see increasingly in new organizations. This work traces the chronology of prevailing organizing principles, from autocratic to democratic, from military to industrial, bringing a historical perspective to the basic proposition that businesses need to be more purposeful, humanistic, and cooperative in the twenty-first century, reflecting the palpable sense that "something is in the air."

If you find any of this work particularly relevant, we highly recommend picking one of the books and convening a study group of three to six colleagues to read and discuss the book further.

EXERCISE 9.2. PERSONAL REFLECTION

Try taking a break from the work of reading, and free your mind to recall past experiences. In particular, reflect on previous work experiences that "went well" or "were successful." Try this:

> *Close your eyes and recall your work history. For any of the work projects or jobs that went well, recall the kinds of working relationships you had with colleagues, managers, and direct reports. Do you see a correlation between jobs that "went well" and strong Level 2 relationships with work colleagues?*

Memories play tricks on us, there is no doubt about that. Nonetheless, we think it is broadly the case that our memories associate positive work experiences to positive Level 2 work relationships. Compensation, awards, and other tangible benefits may make for strong recollections, but we believe those tend to be secondary, whereas recollections of Level 2 relationships with people—personal benefits—will first come to mind. Pay special attention to whether *personization* was involved and in what way.

Part 2. Homework at Your Desk: Analyzing Your Present Relationships and Planning for Future Relationships

Analyzing your current work relationships and networks from a relational point of view is necessary in order to get a sense of what the different levels mean in your particular organization and where you might wish to do more *personizing*.

EXERCISE 9.3. ANALYZING CURRENT RELATIONSHIPS: ROLE MAPPING

1. Draw your own relational map. On a large sheet of paper put yourself into the center, and draw around yourself the names or titles of people who are connected to you in the sense of *expecting something of you*. These are your "role senders." It is important that you figure out what your present relationship to them is and consider what you want it to be as you look ahead (see Figure 9.1).

2. Where you place your role senders (above, below, or to the side), how far away you place them, and the thickness

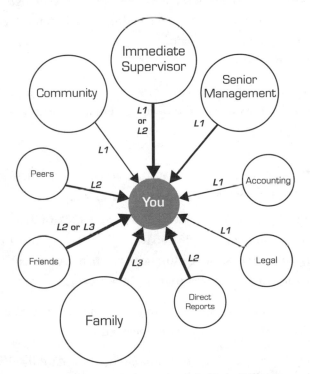

FIGURE 9.1. A Sample Job Role Map

of the arrows from them should reflect your degree of mutually perceived connection.

3. Label each arrow as Level 1, 2, or 3 based on how role-based (1), person-based (2), or intimate (3) you think that relationship is right now.

4. Now focus on those arrows that you labeled Level 2, and on a separate sheet of paper write down what you or they did that enabled the relationship to get to this personal level. Try to remember actual behaviors by you or the other person that seemed to make you "see each other" more as total people, not just roles. Try to identify those behaviors that made you feel more *psychologically safe*, more open, and more trusting in each of those relationships. These behaviors are examples of *personizing* in your own work experience.

5. Identify what those behaviors have in common, and ask yourself how they could be applied in a work situation with a new boss, direct report, or team member.

EXERCISE 9.4. DESIGNING YOUR WORK RELATIONSHIPS AND PREPARING FOR CHANGES IN LEVEL

Think of a person at work with whom you want to build a Level 2 relationship, and prepare a list of what you can do, ask, reveal, and so forth to start that process. Before you spring into action, develop the right mindset:

■ Try to access or become mindful of *unconscious biases* within you toward the other person.

■ Access your ignorance—initially you may actually *know nothing* about the other person.

■ Mobilize your *curiosity* about that person.

In addition, develop the right attitude and motivation:

- I want to get to know *you* as a whole person as quickly as possible.

- I do *not* want to judge you.

- I do *not* want to diagnose you or figure you out.

- I do *not* want to test you.

- I am *curious* about you.

- I want to know *your story*.

- I want to be able to *see* you, that is, to understand a bit about you, to develop a bit of empathy.

Having thought about this and prepared yourself, what are your behavioral choices? Anticipate what *personization* would look like in action. What skills have to be honed or developed?

Part 3. Enhancement of Behavioral Skills

We have pointed out that most of us know how to *personize* in our social and personal activities. You already have the skills, but because you may never have used them in the work setting, you may have to think about what they are, practice them, and hone them for this new application.

EXERCISE 9.5. *PERSONIZATION* BY ASKING OR REVEALING (EITHER APPROACH CAN WORK)

Everything happens through conversation. If you are starting a conversation with a new person and want to *personize* it, what are your options and choices? The basic choice is whether to begin by asking something more personal than usual or by revealing something more personal than usual. As the conversation progresses, this choice will be made by you and the other person repeatedly and naturally. There is no formula. You will have to trust your intuition. The two lists below make some suggestions, but you will have to follow your impulses and personal comfort level to decide which way to go, from moment to moment.

If you begin by *asking questions* of another person,

- Begin with questions that are culturally legitimate to ask of a stranger.

- Life history is an excellent entrée into the person's story: "Where are you from?"

- Ask questions that elicit a narrative: "How did you get here?"

- If generalizations are given, ask for examples.

- Listen for things that are personal, unique not general.

- Respond with interest but be culturally appropriate.

- Allow yourself to follow your curiosity by going down new paths.

If you begin by *revealing yourself* to another person,

- Tell something personal about yourself to start the conversation.

- Watch to see whether the person is interested and is hearing you.

- Reveal more or switch to questioning mode.

- The ideal conversation will have you both asking and revealing.

Body language can be important. There is no formula for this, especially since different cultures attach different meanings to eye contact, physical distance between people in conversation, and overall body posture. However, as our Example 1.5 illustrated, when the surgeon maintained intense eye contact and a body posture that signaled intensity of feeling that the checklist was to be taken seriously, this provided an immediate opportunity for *personization*.

With each exchange you will have a feeling of either being understood and accepted or not, and you can then use those perceptions and feelings to take the next step. It is a mutual learning process, which may involve missteps, awkwardness, or embarrassment, but figure that in this kind of learning, errors are inevitable, so you have to learn from them. You will also have reactions to what the other person is telling you, and those will guide you on whether you want to build the relationship to a deeper level or not. In practice this all happens very rapidly, but you can try to become mindful of your own reactions and feelings as guides for what to say or do next.

EXERCISE 9.6. THE EMPATHY WALK: A REAL CHALLENGE, TOUGH TO DO, AND GENUINELY EYE OPENING

Most of our experience in building relationships occurs in settings where the cultural rules are fairly clear because we are in prescribed roles and are usually building a relationship with someone similar to ourselves in terms of national culture, status, and social class. To have the experience of

Exercise 9.6 was originally developed for a management training program by Richard Walton and Ed Schein.

how difficult this is when you are dealing with someone different on these dimensions, try the following:

Step 1. Find a partner, such as a spouse, friend, or work colleague.

Step 2. Take a half hour or so to consider ways in which you and the partner are most similar in terms of background, experience, occupation, social status, education, nationality, and whatever else occurs to you.

Step 3. Now, both of you try to think of some kind of person in your neighborhood, city, or local area who is *most different from you*. This requires some creativity and some reflection. Also think ahead that your challenge will be to find such a person and establish a relationship with him or her.

Step 4. Find such a person and strike up a conversation with him or her. This is difficult and requires some courage and ingenuity (that's the point!). The key is to figure out how to start to build a relationship without being too invasive.

Step 5. Spend some time with this person to get to know him or her, for about an hour.

Step 6. You and your partner reflect on several questions:
- In what ways did your interviewee turn out to be different?
- What were the hardest parts of developing the relationship?
- Was it even hard for you and your partner to discover your similarities?
- What have you learned about relationship building?

EXERCISE 9.7. REVIEWING THE JOB ROLE MAP—TAPPING EMPATHY TO BECOME MORE HUMBLE AT WORK

Step 1. Go back to your job role map (Figure 9.1), and identify a link that you now think should move to Level 2.

Step 2. Plan a meeting with that person, and make a plan for yourself on how you will either ask questions or reveal things about yourself to deepen the relationship.

Step 3. Throughout the conversation calibrate your own feelings and observe closely the reactions of the other person.

Step 4. Find someone to tell about the experience and help you reflect on what you learned.

Developing Insight into Group Process

So far we have talked about what you can do to develop and enhance one-on-one relationships at work. But what of developing insight into group process and developing the skills to improve meetings, teams, and networks? For this, you may need to *find workshops* in which you get *direct personal experience as a participant.* Here are three organizations that may provide such experiential workshops:

- National Training Laboratories, www.ntl.org; look for "Human Interaction Laboratory"

- Presencing Insitute, https://www.presencing.org/#/programs/marketplace/category/foundation_programs

- Society for Organizational Learning, https://www.solonline.org/foundations-for-leadership-2018/

Interest in group dynamics is slowly building, so there may be other organizations that you can locate through networking and searching online. The important criterion in choosing a workshop is that it is *experiential* and involves some T-group experience.

Summary and Conclusions

Humble Leadership is, in the end, about evolving from Level 1 transactional culture to *personized* Level 2 culture:

FROM Level 1 Culture	TO Level 2 Culture
The person in charge needs to be in control, even if that puts constraints on autonomy and creativity and may stifle engagement and commitment.	The person in charge needs to be a convener/director who encourages autonomy and creativity, even if that limits control of the details but may build enthusiasm and commitment.
Focus on getting the organization design and structure right.	Focus on creating viable and effective relationships and group processes between the structural elements. In other words, focus on the catalysts needed to make the structure work.
Work is accomplished by individuals doing their assigned jobs properly.	Work is accomplished by groups who learn together to perform as an ensemble in which everyone is inspired to contribute wherever they can.
Work is accomplished by following plans, procedures, instructions, and rules of engagement.	Work adapts in order to leverage collective tacit knowledge based on practice, situational awareness, and experimentation.
To innovate, seek out ways to disrupt in order to change markets and work processes.	To innovate, seek out ways to better understand customers and stakeholders, and look for places to offer adaptations and build resiliency.

FROM Level 1 Culture	TO Level 2 Culture
Every task/project needs an individual in charge who is accountable for success.	**Every task/project needs a convener/ director whose function is to build synergy and make the group accountable for its success.**
Status and authority derive from position and expertise.	**Influence and here-and-now authority derive from "ad hoc designed" roles and the new and better behavior that is triggered in the workgroup.**
Leaders establish a strong direction, hold to it, and show no signs of wavering, in order to maintain control, consistency, and commitment.	**Humble leaders embrace ambiguity and work to shrink distance between opposing sides, to achieve shared commitment built on openness and trust.**
Meetings should be efficient (short) and well planned, with clear agendas and preassigned preparation.	**Meetings vary in length and congru- ence with the complexity of the issues to be resolved and the roles and relevance of group members in attendance.**
Meetings need to stick to the agenda and disregard side issues.	**Meetings need to periodically stop the agenda to reflect on the decision process (goal alignment, participation levels, consensus testing).**
Innovation is through a linear sequence of rejecting old processes, brainstorming, ideating, beta testing, and controlled off-line evaluation.	**Innovation is through iteration, thinking while working, allowing new ideas to come from anywhere at any time, and improvising processes in line and in the here and now.**
Get it done, fast, and get it done in whatever way works.	**Get it done in a way that builds agility, repeatability, and learning capacity for the next challenge.**
Make every effort to be heard, to speak up in meetings, and to demonstrate your value.	**Make every effort to listen and "see" others before professing and arguing for yourself.**

FROM Level 1 Culture	TO Level 2 Culture
New ideas come from creative individuals and should be evaluated by critical discussion and interrogation to ensure validity.	New ideas that are possibly worth pursuing are co-created by building on what any individuals might propose in a cooperative rather than confrontational manner.
Build a network for personal advantage.	Build agile, flexible relationships (learning groups) within and across networks.
Reflecting is inward about oneself.	Reflecting is outward about others.
Spend your work time getting things done right.	Spend time reflecting on whether you are doing the right things.
Improve efficiency.	Develop resilient effectiveness.
Maintain professional distance.	Encourage openness and trust

Humble Leadership means accepting vulnerability and building resiliency through **Level 2** relationships.

References

Adams, G. B., & Balfour, D. L. (2009) *Unmasking Administrative Evil.* Armonk, NY: M. E. Sharpe.

Bales, R. F., & Cohen, S. P. (1979) *SYMLOG.* Glencoe, IL: The Free Press.

Barrett, F. J. (2012) *Yes to the Mess.* Cambridge, MA: Harvard Business School Press.

Bennis, W. G., & Shepard, H. A. (1956) "A theory of group development." *Human Relations,* 9, 415–443.

Bion, W. R. (1959) *Experiences in Groups.* London, UK: Tavistock.

Blanchard, K. (2003) *The Servant Leader.* Nashville, TN: Thomas Nelson.

Blanchard, K., & Broadwell, R. (2018) *Servant Leadership in Action.* Oakland, CA: Berrett-Koehler.

Bohm, D. (1989) *On Dialogue.* Ojai, CA: David Bohm Seminars.

Carlson, G. (2017) *Be Fierce.* New York: Center Street.

Edmondson, A. (2012) *Teaming: How Organizations Learn, Innovate, and Compete in the Knowledge Economy.* San Francisco, CA: Jossey-Bass, Wiley.

Edmondson, A., Bohmer, R. M., & Pisano, G. P. (2001) "Disrupted routines: Team learning and new technology implementation in hospitals." *Administrative Science Quarterly,* 46, 685–716.

Farrow, R. (2017) "From aggressive overtures to sexual assault: Harvey Weinstein's accusers tell their stories." *The New Yorker,* October 10.

Friedman, T. (2016) *Thank You for Being Late.* New York: Farrar, Straus and Giroux.

Fussell, C. (2017) *One Mission.* New York: Macmillan.

Gawande, A. (2014) *Being Mortal.* New York: Holt Metropolitan Books.

Gerstein, M. (2008) *Flirting with Disaster.* New York: Union Square.

Gerstein, M. S., & Schein, E. H. (2011) "Dark secrets: Face-work, organizational culture and disaster prevention." In C. de Franco & C. O. Meyer, eds. *Forecasting, Warning and Responding to Transnational Risks*. London: Palgrave Macmillan, pp. 148–165.

Gittell, J. H. (2016) *Transforming Relationships for High Performance: The Power of Relational Coordination*. Stanford, CA: Stanford University Press.

Goffman, E. (1959) *The Presentation of Self in Everyday Life*. New York: Doubleday Anchor.

Goffman, E. (1963) *Behavior in Public Places*. New York: Free Press.

Goffman, E. (1967) *Interaction Ritual*. New York: Pantheon.

Grabell, M. (2017) "Exploitation and abuse at the chicken plant." *The New Yorker*, May 8, pp. 46–53.

Grant, A. (2013) *Give and Take*. New York: Penguin Books.

Greenleaf, R. K. (2002) *Servant Leadership: A Journey into the Nature of Legitimate Power and Greatness* (25th anniversary ed.). New York: Paulist Press.

Hackman, R. (2002) *Leading Teams*. Boston, MA: Harvard Business School Press.

Harvey, J. B. (1988) *The Abilene Paradox and Other Meditations on Management*. Lexington, MA: Lexington Books.

Heifetz, R. A. (1994) *Leadership without Easy Answers*. Cambridge, MA: Harvard University Press.

Isaacs, W. (1999) *Dialogue and the Art of Thinking Together*. New York: Doubleday Currency.

Johansen, B. (2017) *The New Leadership Literacies: Thriving in a Future of Extreme Disruption and Distributed Everything*. Oakland, CA: Berrett-Koehler.

Kahneman, D. (2011) *Thinking Fast and Slow*. New York: Farrar, Strauss & Giro.

Kenney, C. (2011) *Transforming Health Care*. New York: CRC Press.

Kornacki, M. J. (2015) *A New Compact: Aligning Physician-Organization Expectations to Transform Patient Care*. Chicago: Health Administration Press.

Laloux, F. (2014) *Reinventing Organizations: A Guide to Creating Organizations Inspired by the Next Stage of Human Consciousness*. Nelson Parker.

Laloux, F., & Appert, E. (2016) *Reinventing Organizations: An Illustrated Invitation to Join the Conversation on Next-Stage Organizations*. Nelson Parker.

Marquet, L. D. (2012) *Turn the Ship Around*. New York: Portfolio/Penguin.

McChrystal, S. (2015) *Team of Teams: New Rules of Engagement for a Complex World*. New York: Portfolio/Penguin.

McGregor, D. (1960) *The Human Side of Enterprise*. New York: McGraw-Hill.

Nelson, E. C., Batalden, P. B., & Godfrey, M. M. (2007) *Quality by Design*. New York: Wiley.

O'Reilly, C. A. III, & Tushman, M. L. (2016) *Lead and Disrupt*. Stanford, CA: Stanford University Press.

Peh Shing Huei (2016) *Neither Civil Nor Servant: The Philip Yeo Story*. Singapore: Straits Times Press.

Pfeffer, J. (2010) *Power: Why Some People Have It and Some People Don't*. New York: Harper Business.

Plsek, P. (2014) *Accelerating Health Care Transformation with Lean and Innovation*. New York: CRC Press.

Powell, M., & Gifford, J. (2016) *Perform to Win*. London: LID Publishing.

Ricci, R., & Weise, C. (2011) *The Collaboration Imperative: Executive Strategies for Unlocking Your Organization's True Potential*. San Jose, CA: Cisco Systems.

Roth, G., & Kleiner, A. (2000) *Car Launch*. New York: Oxford University Press.

Roy, H. (1970) *The Cultures of Management*. Baltimore: Johns Hopkins University Press.

Scharmer, C. O. (2009) *Theory U*. Oakland, CA: Berrett-Koehler.

Schein, E. H. (1956) "The Chinese indoctrination program for Prisoners of War: A study of attempted brainwashing." *Psychiatry*, 19, 149–172.

Schein, E. H. (1989) "Reassessing the 'Divine Rights' of managers." *Sloan Management Review*, 30(2), 63–68.

Schein, E. H. (1996) *Strategic Pragmatism*. Cambridge, MA: MIT Press.

Schein, E. H. (1999) *Process Consultation Revisited*. Reading, MA: Addison-Wesley.

Schein, E. H. (2003) *DEC Is Dead: Long Live DEC*. Oakland, CA: Berrett-Koehler.

Schein, E. H. (2009) *Helping*. Oakland, CA: Berret-Koehler.

Schein, E. H. (2013a) *Humble Inquiry*. Oakland, CA: Berret-Koehler.

Schein, E. H. (2013b) "The culture factor in safety culture." In G. Grote & J. S. Carroll, eds. *Safety Management in Context*. ETH,

Zurich & MIT, Cambridge, MA: Swiss Re Centre for Global Dialogue, pp. 75–80.

Schein, E. H. (2014) "The role of coercive persuasion in education and learning: Subjugation or animation?" In *Research in Organizational Change and Development*, Volume 22. Emerald Group Publishing, pp. 1–23.

Schein, E. H. (2016) *Humble Consulting*. Oakland, CA: Berrett-Koehler.

Schein, E. H., & Bennis, W. G. (1965) *Personal and Organizational Change through Group Methods: The Laboratory Approach.* New York: Wiley.

Schein, E. H., & Schein, P. A. (2017) *Organizational Culture and Leadership* (5th ed.). New York: Wiley.

Seelig, J. (2017) *Thank you America: A memoir.* Palo Alto, CA. (unpublished).

Senge, P. M. (1990) *The Fifth Discipline.* New York: Doubleday Currency.

Senge, P. M., Roberts, C., Ross, R. B., Smith, B. J., & Kleiner, A. (1994) *The Fifth Discipline Field Book.* New York: Doubleday Currency.

Sennett, R. (2006) *The Culture of the New Capitalism.* New Haven, CT: Yale University Press.

Shook, J. (2000) *Managing to Learn.* Cambridge, MA: The Lean Enterprise Institute.

Silversin, J., & Kornacki, M. J. (2000) *Leading Physicians through Change.* Tampa, FL: ACPE. (Second edition, 2012).

Sutton, R. (2007) *The No Asshole Rule: Building a Civilized Workplace and Surviving One That Isn't.* New York: Warner Business Books Hachette Book Group USA.

Swisher, K. (2013) "Physically together: Here's the internal Yahoo no-work-from-home memo for remote workers and maybe more." New York: *All Things D / The Wall Street Journal*, February 22, 2014.

Valentine, M. (2017) "When Equity seems unfair: The role of justice enforceability in temporary team coordination." *Academy of Management Journal.* On line, 10/03/17.

Valentine, M. A., & Edmondson, A. C. (2015) "Team scaffolds: How mesolevel structures enable role-based coordination in temporary groups." *Organization Science* 26(2), 405–422.

Vaughan, D. (1996) *The* Challenger *Launch Decision: Risky Technology, Culture and Deviance at NASA.* Chicago: University of Chicago Press.

Venable, J. V. (2016) *Breaking the Trust Barrier.* Oakland, CA: Berrett-Koehler.

Weick, K. E. (1995) *Sensemaking in Organizations.* Thousand Oaks, CA: Sage.

Weick, K. E., & Sutcliffe, K. M. (2007) *Managing the Unexpected.* San Francisco, CA: Jossey-Bass, Wiley.

Acknowledgments

This book has a long history. For Ed it goes back to what he learned from his mentor and boss, Douglas McGregor, in his very first job at MIT in 1956. The essence of Humble Leadership was learned from Doug through his classic book *The Human Side of Enterprise* (1960) and his personal behavior as a leader.

Humble leaders we have known throughout our careers are for Ed some of his clients: Ken Olsen at Digital Equipment Corporation, Sam Koechlin at Ciba-Geigy, Gene McGrath at Con Edison, James Ellis at the Institute for Nuclear Power Operations, and Gary Kaplan at Virginia Mason Health Center. For Peter, key influential leaders include Ted West at Pacific Bell, James Isaacs and Chris Bryant at Apple, Jan Tyler Bock at Silicon Graphics, Inc., and Brian Sutphin and Jonathan Schwartz at Sun Microsystems, Inc.

Ed's colleagues, the late Warren Bennis, Lotte Bailyn, John Van Maanen, Bob McKersie, John Carroll, and Otto Scharmer, were exemplars of *personizing*. Ed learned from them by identifying with their humility and curiosity as teachers and colleagues. He learned how to be a humble leader in complex situations from the late Richard Beckhard, a veritable genius at *personizing* with colleagues and clients.

The many OD colleagues past and present who have been influential are listed in alphabetical order: Michael and

Linda Brimm, Warner Burke, Gervaise Bushe, Rosa Carrillo, John Cronkite, Tina Doerffer, Gerhard Fatzer, Mei Lin Fung, Kathryn Schulyer Goldman, Charles Handy, David Jamieson, Bob Marshak, Joanne Martin, Henry Mintzberg, Philip Mix, Peter Sorensen, Ilene Wasserman, and Therese Yaeger, as well as David Bradford with whom Ed has wrestled out some of these ideas over intense lunches. Our philosopher friend Noam Cook forced us to think clearly about individualism and groups. Amy Edmondson, Jody Gittell, and Kathy MacDonald helped greatly in working through some of the semantics of "levels of relationship."

Peter's perspective has been deeply informed by key faculty at the Human Capital and Effective Organizations program at USC Marshall School of Business, in particular Chris Worley, Ed Lawler, Sue Mohrman, Jon Boudreau, Alec Levenson, and Soren Kaplan.

In our joint effort with our Organizational Culture and Leadership Institute (OCLI.org) over the last 2 years we learned a great deal from clients and colleagues in the organization development field. Many of them influenced this project directly by their questions, their responses to our earlier works *Humble Inquiry* (Schein, 2013a) and *Humble Consulting* (Schein, 2016), and their encouragement, especially Rob Cooke and Tim Kuppler at Human Synergistics, Lucian Leape, James and Joy Hereford at Stanford Health, Mary Jane Kornacki and Jack Silversin at Amicus, Diane Rawlins and Tony Suchman with whom we evolved a workshop on health care, Marjorie Godfrey, Jeff Richardson, Lynne Ware, Adrienne Seal, Michelle Sullivan, Kimberly Wiefling, and the faculty and students of the last several classes of the Pepperdine University OD program. Ed also learned a great deal from his close colleague at Alliant University Jo Sanzgiri, her partner Julie Bertucelli, and her student Manisha Bajaj, with whom he formed a training group to explore group process more deeply. He also benefited from the research of Yifat Sharabi-Levine on the use of CEO power, and appreciated the wonderful role modeling of Humble Leadership displayed by Dr. Wally Krengel.

Overseas colleagues with whom we have worked on these ideas are Lily and Peter Cheng in Singapore, Michael Chen in Shanghai, and especially Joichi Ogawa, who has become a close colleague in the process of introducing our work into Japan over the last 15 years.

We have also had opportunities to test some of these ideas at the Organization Design Forum and there worked closely with Mary and Stu Winby, Claudia Murphy, and Sue Mohrman. Similarly, we much appreciate Bob Johansen at the Institute for the Future for his counsel and the opportunity to discuss our ideas with some of his clients.

As with other books, we owe a great debt to Steve Piersanti, our editor and publisher. Without his guidance, and that of Jeevan Sivasubramaniam, this book would not have been possible.

Finally, we acknowledge our closest family members, Louisa Schein, Liz Krengel, and especially Jamie Schein, as well as Ed's grandchildren, who have heard, reacted to, challenged, and improved our thinking about the implications of Humble Leadership *in the future* that they will experience and shape for generations to come.

Index

About the Authors

Ed Schein is Professor Emeritus of the Massachusetts Institute of Technology (MIT) Sloan School of Management. He was educated at the University of Chicago, Stanford University, and Harvard University, where he received his PhD in Social Psychology in 1952. He worked at the Walter Reed Institute of Research for 4 years and then joined MIT, where he taught until 2005. He has published extensively—*Organizational Psychology*, 3rd ed. (1980); *Process Consultation Revisited* (1999); *Career Anchors*, 4th ed. (with John Van Maanen, 2013; on career dynamics); *Organizational Culture and Leadership*, 5th ed. (2017); *The Corporate Culture Survival Guide*, 2nd ed. (2009); on a cultural analysis of Singapore's economic miracle (*Strategic Pragmatism*, 1996); and on the rise and fall of Digital Equipment Corp. (*DEC Is Dead; Long Live DEC*, 2003).

In 2009 he published *Helping*, a book on the general theory and practice of giving and receiving help, followed in 2013 by *Humble Inquiry*, which explores why helping is so difficult in Western culture and which won the 2013 business book of the year award from the Dept. of Leadership of the University of San Diego. He published *Humble Consulting* in 2016, which revises the whole model of how to consult and coach, and is working with his son Peter on various projects in their Organizational Culture and Leadership Institute (OCLI.org).

He is the 2009 recipient of the Distinguished Scholar-Practitioner Award of the Academy of Management, the 2012 recipient of the Lifetime Achievement Award from the International Leadership Association, and the 2015 Lifetime Achievement Award in Organization Development from the International OD Network and has an Honorary Doctorate from the IEDC Bled School of Management in Slovenia.

Peter Schein is the cofounder and COO of OCLI.org in Menlo Park, CA. He provides counsel to senior management on organizational development challenges facing private and public sector entities worldwide. He is a contributing author to the 5th edition of *Organizational Culture and Leadership* (Schein, 2017).

Peter's work draws on 30 years of industry experience in marketing and corporate development at technology pioneers. In his early career he developed new products at Pacific Bell and Apple. He led new product efforts at Silicon Graphics, Inc., Concentric Network Corporation (XO

Communications), and Packeteer (Blue Coat). Thereafter, Peter spent 11 years in corporate development and strategy at Sun Microsystems, where he led numerous investments in high-growth ecosystems. He drove acquisitions of technology innovators that developed into highly valued product lines at Sun. Through these experiences developing new strategies organically, and merging smaller entities into a large company, Peter developed a keen focus on the underlying organizational development challenges that growth engenders in innovation-driven enterprises.

Peter was educated at Stanford University (BA Social Anthropology, with Honors and Distinction), Northwestern University (Kellogg MBA, Marketing and Information Management), and the USC Marshall School of Business (HCEO Certificate).

Other titles by Edgar Schein in the Humble Leadership Series

Humble Inquiry
The Gentle Art of Asking Instead of Telling

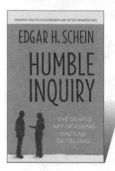

To generate bold new ideas, to avoid disastrous mistakes, to develop agility and flexibility, we need to practice Humble Inquiry. In this seminal work (130,000 copies sold worldwide and translated into thirteen languages), Schein contrasts Humble Inquiry with other kinds of inquiry, shows the benefits it provides, and offers advice on overcoming the cultural, organizational, and psychological barriers that keep us from practicing it.

Paperback, 144 pages, ISBN 978-1-60994-981-5
PDF ebook, ISBN 978-1-60994-982-2
ePub ebook ISBN 978-1-60994-983-9

Humble Consulting
How to Provide Real Help Faster

Schein argues that consultants have to jettison the old idea of professional distance and work with their clients in a more personal way, emphasizing authentic openness, curiosity, and humility. He draws deeply on his own decades of experience, offering over two dozen case studies that illuminate each stage of this Humble Consulting process.

Paperback, 240 pages, ISBN 978-1-62656-720-7
PDF ebook, ISBN 978-1-62656-721-4
ePub ebook ISBN 978-1-62656-722-1
Digital audio ISBN 978-1-62656-724-5

BK Berrett–Koehler Publishers, Inc.
www.bkconnection.com **800.929.2929**

Berrett–Koehler
Publishers

Berrett-Koehler is an independent publisher dedicated to an ambitious mission: *Connecting people and ideas to create a world that works for all.*

We believe that the solutions to the world's problems will come from all of us, working at all levels: in our organizations, in our society, and in our own lives. Our BK Business books help people make their organizations more humane, democratic, diverse, and effective (we don't think there's any contradiction there). Our BK Currents books offer pathways to creating a more just, equitable, and sustainable society. Our BK Life books help people create positive change in their lives and align their personal practices with their aspirations for a better world.

All of our books are designed to bring people seeking positive change together around the ideas that empower them to see and shape the world in a new way.

And we strive to practice what we preach. At the core of our approach is Stewardship, a deep sense of responsibility to administer the company for the benefit of all of our stakeholder groups including authors, customers, employees, investors, service providers, and the communities and environment around us. Everything we do is built around this and our other key values of quality, partnership, inclusion, and sustainability.

This is why we are both a B-Corporation and a California Benefit Corporation—a certification and a for-profit legal status that require us to adhere to the highest standards for corporate, social, and environmental performance.

We are grateful to our readers, authors, and other friends of the company who consider themselves to be part of the BK Community. We hope that you, too, will join us in our mission.

A BK Business Book

We hope you enjoy this BK Business book. BK Business books pioneer new leadership and management practices and socially responsible approaches to business. They are designed to provide you with groundbreaking and practical tools to transform your work and organizations while upholding the triple bottom line of people, planet, and profits. High-five!

To find out more, visit **www.bkconnection.com**.

Berrett–Koehler
Publishers

Connecting people and ideas
to create a world that works for all

Dear Reader,

Thank you for picking up this book and joining our worldwide community of Berrett-Koehler readers. We share ideas that bring positive change into people's lives, organizations, and society.

To welcome you, we'd like to offer you a free e-book. You can pick from among twelve of our bestselling books by entering the promotional code **BKP92E** here: http://www.bkconnection.com/welcome.

When you claim your free e-book, we'll also send you a copy of our e-newsletter, the *BK Communiqué*. Although you're free to unsubscribe, there are many benefits to sticking around. In every issue of our newsletter you'll find

- A free e-book
- Tips from famous authors
- Discounts on spotlight titles
- Hilarious insider publishing news
- A chance to win a prize for answering a riddle

Best of all, our readers tell us, "Your newsletter is the only one I actually read." So claim your gift today, and please stay in touch!

Sincerely,

Charlotte Ashlock
Steward of the BK Website

Questions? Comments? Contact me at bkcommunity@bkpub.com.

Certified

Corporation
bcorporation.net